D1085818

10 LESSONS

IN

COACHING

Leadership Lessons from a Career in Coaching and Athletic Administration

By

Chris Parker

ISBN: 978-1-09833-282–2

This book is dedicated to my family. My wife, Kimberly, and my daughters, Ellie and Kate. They sacrificed seeing me for years so I could learn these lessons in coaching and athletic administration.

Table of Contents

Introduction

I walked into a conference room in early January 2008 at Chapel Hill High School in Douglasville, GA. I was too ignorant to realize that I should have been honored to even be considered for their Head Football Coaching job. I was young. I was too arrogant to care that the team was coming off an 0-10 season and had only won 15 of the 80 varsity football games the school had ever played. It was one of those strange times where ignorance and arrogance may have been beneficial.

I still have no idea why they picked me, but they did! I was so excited! Just like that, I am the leader of a "program". This is more than just a team; it is a program. It involves hundreds of people and moving parts. I thought I was ready, but quickly realized I was not. The reality settles in fast. Being a leader is a difficult task with many lessons learned. Unfortunately, I learned most of the lessons "the hard way".

I was fortunate to be around good players and good assistant coaches and together we built successful teams. Over the next decade, I was able to lead a football program at 2 different schools, lead a High School Athletic Department and eventually lead a school district's entire Athletic Department. As I write this, I am a school district Director of Human

Resources. Each of these roles has taught me a great deal about leadership.

The pages of this book include some of the lessons I have learned during my career in coaching and athletics administration. Everyone talks about problems. I want to talk about solutions. I want to talk about REAL solutions. I hope this book gives you some advice on HOW to do things to help your program. I feel like it is easy to say generic statements, but when do we lay out ways and methods on how to implement ideas? What I will attempt to do in this book is take some basic, generic lessons and show you how to apply them to common problems that arise in leadership. I hope this will be helpful for veteran and aspiring leaders alike.

The Lessons

"Half the teams have to lose." This was a common quote used in our practices for years. No one intentionally fails at their leadership job, but half of the leaders will fail in all contests. I have found that most people in leadership roles consider themselves good leaders. Unfortunately, we know that cannot be true. I considered myself a good leader in 2008 when I became the head coach. I had a long way to go and each year I felt like I was a much better leader than the year before. Everyone can be a better leader. Regardless of what type of leader you consider yourself, take these 10 lessons and learn them now. I had to learn many the hard way!

Teachers study to learn how to teach. Student teaching, teaching cohorts, and other education classes are great tools for current and future educators. I always found it interesting that coaching was somewhat frowned upon in these educational settings. There was little, if any, preparation for being a coach in the education process. Teachers usually had to agree to coach or sponsor something to get their first job and they had no training. Parents, administrators, and athletes immediately expected the coach to know what to do regardless if they were inexperience and had little training. I have recently felt a need to help fill this coaching educational void and help the best way I can. I do not have all the answers, but I have learned a lot over the years and would like to share what I have learned with you.

Consider these lessons one of many tools you can use to help yourself get in that good "half" each game! Hopefully, it will help your program succeed more and in turn you will make more of a difference in the lives of those around you.

Lesson One:

Put Relationships over Everything

The truth is if you do not understand this first "Lesson" the others really do not matter. If you are not willing to focus on relationships and put relationships above everything else, you will not be successful as a coach. It really is that simple. Relationships with players, assistant coaches, administration, parents, and others will all determine how successful you will be as a leader.

As you build positive relationships with the people around you, you will gradually gain their respect. This respect will feed your success as a leader. When you earn respect, you will be able to talk to a person about anything. The individual will listen and value your opinion. A successful leader needs a trusting relationship with each person in the organization to get them to put the team first. One of the keys to being successful is managing the critical conversations.

The ability to have a crucial conversation with someone may be one of the most underrated traits necessary for successful leadership. People reveal their level of respect for you when you tell them something they do NOT want to hear. It seems that "back in the day" you could get respect just by having the "Head Coach" title. Now you must earn that respect. You earn respect through the relationships you build over time.

I have not met anyone that did not want to build good relationships. No one intentionally messes this up. While being a builder of relationships is something that some people are naturally better at than others, it is also a learned behavior. Always work on building better relationships. The work is never done and there is always a new person to help!

The relationships you build will determine how you handle these situations:
- Convincing players to buy in to the team first
- Turning a losing program around
- Maintaining a winning program
- Upset parents
- Assistant coach issues
- Administration issues
- Team Culture issues

> ➤ Convincing parents/players you are doing your best in college recruiting
> ➤ Player discipline
> ➤ Parent participation
> ➤ Outside influences trying to lure players to other places

How can you get better at building relationships? Here are the important factors:

- ✓ Show them you care
- ✓ Get to know them
- ✓ Be honest with them
- ✓ Put yourself in their shoes
- ✓ Be there for them

Show them you care

You cannot be scared to show people you care about them. This was a mistake many coaches made years ago. Be yourself and, although it is overused and cliché, treat everyone the way you would like to be treated. Be proud of people on your team when they do something good. Take every opportunity you can to brag on someone in your program. Make sure your care is genuine. Fake is easy to spot. Genuine, real care is a powerful thing. If someone knows you care about them, they will listen to you when you have something to say. The old saying, "they don't care how much you know until they know how much you care" is true.

Recognition matters to people now. If you do not like it, you will have to get over it as I am afraid it is here to stay. When I first started coaching, I hated recognitions. I believed you should do good things and work hard for the team and not to get recognized. As I grew as a head football coach, my philosophy on this evolved. As times have changed and social media became more important, I felt forced to pick between what I liked to do or what I needed to do to win. The expansion of the internet and social media completely changed the landscape. It was not my job to judge whether that was good or bad. It was my job to help the people on our team reach their maximum potential. I wanted every player and coach to feel like they were better because they were part of our program. It became evident we needed to recognize our players more and we needed to teach them more character traits than they were learning. We developed a Team Building program.

We would start practice on Mondays and Tuesdays in the locker room having a group discussion. On Wednesday we would not have a pre-practice discussion and go straight out to practice. At the end of Wednesday practice, we would get everyone together and give out "helmet stickers". These helmet stickers became a staple of our program and was a way we could show them we cared.

We would start out the team meeting each Wednesday evening having each assistant coach give out 1 or 2 helmet stickers from the last week. The coaches would pick a mix of young players and older players who stood out either in the game or in practices. I would always go last as the Head Coach and I would give out several. I tried to give them out for intangible reasons and make sure I recognized people and things that many would not recognize. Things like playing hard on the scout team, giving great effort in individual parts of practice or in the weight room. I also always recognized a couple young players for their hard work.

We even let the teachers get in on the fun. On Wednesday mornings I would usually send an email to the faculty and ask them who they wanted to give a helmet sticker. This was a hit. Teachers would respond with people who were doing well in their class. I would have a list and I would read off which teachers gave out stickers to what players. The players loved it. They would go to class and beg teachers to get a helmet sticker. Teachers responded to me that they had seen an increase in positive behavior with some athletes because of helmet stickers. It was a great way for the teachers to show they cared to the athletes.

Finally, we would let the players give out helmet stickers. Players would select other players who they thought stood out during the week. They would stand up and say who they wanted to give the sticker to and for what reason. Everyone clapped for each person. We had to limit it each week to usually around 10 stickers. At least one of those stickers needed to be given by a player to another player for something they did outside of the field. We heard some good things that players said about other players in the classroom and in the community. It was a thing that really made our team closer.

As the Athletic Director and Head Football Coach I was usually charged with being the "administrator on duty" at our basketball games. I was not much help to cover games in the fall so I enjoyed attending our basketball games. I would always make a point to go see the football players that were in attendance and talk to them. At one particular game I had one of our freshman football players come up to me and show me the back of his cell phone where he had placed the helmet sticker that I gave him a few months earlier. He had taken it off his helmet after the season and stuck it on his phone so he could keep it. He told me, "I was prouder of this than anything else, Coach!" I was genuinely amazed at how much that meant to him. It took little effort from me, but it meant a great deal to him. That is just one instance of many times players told me stories about how they got a helmet sticker. Those little helmet stickers meant a lot!

<u>Show them you care: How do you do it?</u>

- ✓ **Take advantage of every opportunity to brag on someone** – do not be "too cool" to say nice things about people. They need to hear nice things when they do something well. Positive reinforcement is a real thing!

- ✓ **Have a rewards and awards system** – you do not have to use helmet stickers but find something where you can reward and award people for doing good things.

- ✓ **Recognize birthdays** – I always kept a running list of everyone in our organization and recognize their birthdays. You can do it on social media, or you can simply send them a message wishing them happy birthday. It takes a minute or two a day and it is a great way to show you care.

- ✓ **Embrace the current** – Social Media is a great tool that we did not have when I was starting out in athletics. If you want to show people you care, you must meet them where they are. Whenever the next thing comes around, find that!

Get to know them

Do not treat the people in your program like they are just a part of the puzzle or a person you are using to help "your" program. Make them feel like part of "our" program by genuinely getting to know them. This is another common mistake made by coaches. They accidently treat players like they only matter relative to their value on the field or court. This is a huge mistake. I have not seen many coaches do this on purpose but when you do not have a clear plan to get to know your players, it can happen. Talk to players about their personal lives. Do not make it all about the game.

Team building activities are a great way to get to know people in your organization. These can be formal or informal events. We always had some planned "team events" each year but I thought the best way we addressed this was through our regular team meetings. We would have brief discussions before each Monday and Tuesday practice to discuss what we were doing that day and to discuss a character issue. We tried to put the team members in situations where they must talk to each other. We wanted them to know that we cared about them and they cared about each other. We talked about many topics, but it was always more powerful when the players and assistant coaches talked. At some point in each season, I wanted every player and assistant coach to answer these questions to the entire team:

1. *Why do you play/coach football?*
2. *What does this team mean to you?*

The answers we would get to those two simple questions were amazing. We started by letting most of our players do this in the first few weeks of our fall team camp. All of the coaches would go as well. This exercise provided us with so many moments where players genuinely got to know each other and the person speaking had to reflect on those questions. It is important for everyone to know the answer to these questions. We had some players that just answered with quick and generic answers, but we had some that told of how important the team was to them because of all the hardships they had in their life. These were the most impactful. To see students feeling empathy, compassion, and love for other students after learning about one another was great.

You can do this informally as well. Talk to the people in your program constantly. Get to know them and their interests. Take time to understand what they like away from the game and recognize any accomplishments they may have in those fields. I also always wanted to know what they planned to do after they graduated high school. I wanted to be able to support and help them get there. Of course, many of our players aspired to play in college. That was a dream we wanted to support and find as many places as possible for them to choose from. If they did not aspire to play college football, we still wanted to help them get to the next step in life. The only way to start this process is to get to know them!

Get to know them: How do you do it?
- ✓ **Team Building Activities** – you do not have to do it the same way I did, but make sure you have a plan to talk as a team.

- ✓ **Talk to them all the time** – Always be talking to the people in your program. Build up that good relationship in the good times. Things as simple as saying "Good morning", "How's it going today" make a difference. Speak to the people in your organization.

- ✓ **Get to know their interest, their loved ones, etc.** – make it a point to ask how their family is doing. Make a mental note when they tell you something significant about them and bring it up later.

- ✓ **Recognize accomplishments outside of your team** – recognize things they do that do not involve your organization. People will know you care if you show interest in the things which they show interest. If a player becomes an Eagle Scout, make a big deal about it. If a coach gets married, make a big deal about it. If a player that was struggling does well in school, make a big deal about it. You do not have to put all of this on social media but have at least a private conversation with them to tell them how happy you are for them.

- ✓ **Check on their career status** – whether they aspire to play in college, go to college, or get a job after playing for your team, make sure you ask them and help them toward that goal. Make yourself notes to periodically check on their status.

Be honest with them

It is an exceedingly difficult thing to be able to tell someone something they do not want to hear, but if you can do it your program will be much stronger. If you deceive people to make the conversation easier, it will come back to make more work for you in the long run. Developing a reputation of honesty will pay off. Honesty can compound over time. If players tell other players you are honest with them, it will develop into part of the culture and they will believe you when you tell them your plan.

This comes up often for coaches when players want to play positions that are different than the position the coach sees best. I always handled this the same way: We would let them play where they wanted to play for a period and then re-evaluate. It was important to let them play where they want so they feel like they have a voice and you may be wrong about it. Occasionally a player went to a different position than where I saw them and performed well. I was never upset to be wrong about gaining another good player! Unfortunately, usually I was right, and they were better at the position at which we saw them. When this happened, we could ignore it if possible and let the problem get bigger or we could address it. I would bring the young man in and address him and be honest with what we see in him. It is not always what they want to hear but they do appreciate the honesty.

We had individual meetings at least twice a year with each player in our program. In those meetings, we tried to "see the future" as much as possible and let players know what issues they would have in the coming months. I found that being honest with them in these meetings and letting them know where they stand was difficult in the moment but saved a lot of headaches down the road.

Honesty is a key component in adult relationships. When dealing with parents, it is sometimes much easier to tell them what they want to hear because it allows you to get out of the conversation. It does not make things better. You will have to revisit the conversation later and at that time you will have to have a much more difficult conversation because the issue lingered. Many times, I have seen coaches just tell a parent what they want to hear in the off-season about things like: what position they would play, their prospects at the next level, and more. This is easy to do. You must be like a chess player and think many moves ahead. "Seeing the future", is a key aspect to building positive relationships. You must get the feel for when you need to have a tough conversation with someone. Therefore, it is so important to show them you care and get to know them. If you have bragged on a player and speak to him and his parents all the time, it will be much easier to be honest when telling them something they do not want to hear.

Be honest with them: How do you do it?
- ✓ **Make it a point to let people know where they stand** – have formal or informal meetings with the people in your

organization to let them know what they are doing well and what they can do to improve.

✓ **Think moves ahead** – you must "see the future" and anticipate people being upset, disappointed, and hurt. When you see that coming, go talk to them. Have a tough conversation now to make it much easier later. The alternative is worse!

✓ **Never deceive to make it easier on you** – have the hard conversation early rather than later. Do not get out of a tough conversation by telling someone something you know to be untrue that you will have to deal with later.

Put yourself in their shoes

Try to think of things from the perspective of the other person. Whether it is players, coaches, other sports, administration, or parents, always think of it from their perspective as well as yours. It is ok to disagree. It is not ok to not understand each other. When you are having a critical conversation or must make a decision, try to think about how the other person will feel.

If it is a player, try to remember what you felt like as a player. Too often, we as coaches forget what it was like to be a player. What may seem like an insignificant thing can be a big deal to them. If they are attempting to speak to you and you blow them off that will resonate in a negative way. That will not help build your relationship. This does not mean you have to "give in" to the player, it simply means show some compassion and let them know you understand that they may not agree or understand this decision. When this is done with sincerity, it can be highly effective.

Putting yourself in the other person's shoes is probably most imperative when dealing with administration and the leaders of the other organizations in your school. Every coach, band director, and principal needs to work to push their organization. It is impossible for all of them to all have the same vision all the time. It is at these times, that your relationship will grow or deteriorate with that group or individual. I can remember many times when we needed to compromise with one of these people and it may not have been the best thing for our team that day but it was the best thing to keep our relationship strong.

Put yourself in their shoes: How do you do it?

- ✓ **Be fair and consistent** – the best way to understand what the other person is thinking is to have common stances on issues. They will immediately think it is "unfair". You must be able to explain to them that you understand how they feel but this is the consistent way you have done things for years.

- ✓ **Be compassionate and empathetic** – you can stick to your point and still understand they may not agree. You can show some compassion when making a difficult decision or having a critical conversation.

Be there for them

Always check on the people in your program when they need you. Treat them with the care and compassion you would your own family. Things will not always be great. When people are down, they are aware of who is there for them. It is in these moments that your relationship is either growing or deteriorating.

This is obviously true when you have people on the team that are going through major changes in their life like a death in the family or divorce. People may not seem to care much about you asking about their well being or asking what you can do to help but do it anyway. It does matter. If possible, show up to the viewings or funeral services when people on your team have loved ones that have passed on. Just your presence is a way you can be there for them.

One time that occasionally gets neglected is checking on injured players. I think coaches do a great job of showing sympathy and checking on the major injuries but sometimes accidently tear down their relationship with a player by dismissing a "minor" injury. When you have been coaching for twenty years it is easy to call something "minor" that is not minor to that young person. Maybe they have never been hurt before and they do not understand how to act. Maybe they are scared. Sometimes the coach calling to check on them that evening or the next morning at school will build your relationship with that player more than you realize.

For assistant coaches it becomes more of an issue when they must miss team obligations for family. Never get in the way of this. I would always let our guys do what they needed to do for their families. I saw nothing good coming out of me "taking a stand" against something family related so we could practice. This trait allows you to build that relationship with that coach so you can have critical conversations with them moving forward when necessary.

Be there for them: How do you do it?

- ✓ **Always check on injured players** – regardless of the severity of the injury, call them or find them at school the next day and let them know you care about them and their wellbeing.

- ✓ **Always be there when there is illness/death** – make yourself a note to check on them for a few days and then again after an extended period. Make sure to attend some of the viewing or service if possible.

- ✓ **Be understanding when things come up** – you can build or deteriorate your relationship by how you handle someone when they have the unexpected event that forces them to miss something.

Do not forget the adult relationships

As a coach, it is so important to cultivate the adult relationships. It seems that many coaches immediately attempt to develop relationships with students but struggle with the adults. There is no argument the students are likely more important, but BOTH groups are important in being a successful leader. Building relationships with adults is not limited to assistant coaches. It also includes administration, parents, and the leaders of the other sports and organizations in the school.

I tried to go into each adult relationship with an open mind. Try not to use preconceived notions. Other people are going to tell you their opinions. I tried hard to not let that influence my relationship with the adults in our program. I wanted to only go off what I saw from each individual. Work with each assistant coach, administrator, other sports' coach and get to know them. If you have a plan and build relationships, you can make it work.

This is never more important than when you first take over a leadership position. When I became the Head Football Coach at Pickens High I was able to bring in a few coaches that were familiar with my system but not familiar with the Pickens community and blend those coaches with coaches from the old staff that were very familiar with the community. I was fortunate that my brother always coached with me. I knew I had one person that knew what I wanted to do, but he did not know the Pickens community. The coach who was the longest tenured coach on the previous staff was someone I immediately went to see. He had also wanted the job and sometimes that can cause issues. We hit it off immediately and he has since become one of my best friends. We blended our ideas with their ideas to create a plan that was best for everyone. I really believe this "blending" of the new with the old is one of the main reasons we were able to turn around the struggling program.

Use the same things outlined in this chapter with adults: Show them you care, get to know them, be honest with them, put yourself in their shoes, and be there for them. Sometimes this can be hard with parents. You do have to keep a certain level of professionalism, but you do not have to be rude. You can build relationships with parents by talking to them in the good times. Obviously they will have an issue with you if it affects their child but the amount of respect you have shown them up to that point will have a lot to do with the success of the critical conversation that is coming. I tried to make it a point to speak to parents when attending other sporting events and ask about former players when I saw their parents out. The key is to be genuine. Remember, fake is easy to spot.

Administration is another area where building relationships is so crucial. Your administration should trust you and know you want what is best for students. If they do not, ask yourself if you are only engaging with them when you want something. Make sure you are showing them they can trust you to look out for the entire school and not just the aspect you lead. Ask the administration what you can do to help at school functions like graduation and be a "team player" when they need you to help. Step up and show your care for the entire school.

We tried to have a detailed plan for showing appreciation for all our groups. I made formal and informal efforts to recognize and show appreciation for each assistant coach. I always praised the other sports teams. As a football coach, I struggled showing the appreciation necessary to the band and cheerleaders. I genuinely did appreciate them. I always made it a point do general recognitions and to shake every senior's hand on senior night but I thought we could do better. One day, our band director at Pickens came to me with an idea he had seen some other schools do: we could have a practice where the band members and football team practice together. We would practice football together with football players helping teach the band how to do the drills and football players learn how to march in the band. We invited the cheerleaders as well and turned it into a Football/Band/Cheer Appreciation day for our teams. The event was a huge success! We took one of our last summer workouts in late July when the band would be having band camp and cheer would be preparing for the season and we had practice together. All three groups went together and did football drills (no pads of course), then learned to march and cheer. The kids in all three groups had the best time! We always invited the community, administration, and parents to watch as well. This single event was a great way for all three of our organizations to show the other two how much we appreciated them. (Feel free to take this idea and steal it!)

Keys for relationships with adults

✓ **We are all in this together** – say this mantra and live by it! This is easy to tell others and sometimes hard to tell yourself. You must work with these adults.

✓ **Praise in public and bring up issues in private** – If you have an issue with the band, basketball coach, assistant coach, principal, etc. make sure that you talk to them privately. It could likely be a misunderstanding. Never tear down these people publicly. Always assume they are in the room listening when you are talking about them to parents or community people.

✓ **Recognize the groups for helping you as much as possible** – when the other sports win a big game, congratulate them on social media. When they do anything to help your team, make sure to post it! Thank the other groups as much as possible. Recognize assistant coach accomplishments!

✓ **Try to see things from their point of view** – it can be difficult to do, but it will make things much better for your relationship.

Conclusion

Your job as a leader is to help each person in your program reach their maximum potential so that the program can reach its maximum potential. This will never be accomplished without strong relationships. Put relationship building at the top of your priority list.

Once you understand the importance of relationships, you can start formulating a plan to succeed. In the next chapter, we talk about how to start planning!

Lesson Two:

Have a Plan

After years of doing both, I stopped coaching football after the 2018 season and focused on being the District Athletic Director. At the beginning of 2020, I was moved from District Athletic Director to Director of Human Resources for the district. This move was exciting but also sad as I had been involved with athletics for decades. I did not anticipate this change, and I was told it was "effective immediately". I did not get to have a farewell. I was immediately immersed in an entirely new part of the school system and, although I have thoroughly enjoyed it, there was something missing. Realizing I was likely not going to be involved in athletics, I started posting old coaching responsibilities and plans on Twitter. For years, people have known I was organized and have emailed me wanting our plan for this or that. I got one of these emails right after I was moved to Human Resources. I decided instead of sending it to this particular coach, I would just post it for any coach that wanted it. I was blown away by the results. I had over fifty messages on the first day or two wanting me to email it to them. I started posting parts of our plans daily. It has taken off and is probably one of the reasons you are reading this! The moral of the story is: I had no idea there was such a demand for clear, concise plans.

While I have received a lot of praise for these plans, the reality is plans win zero games. It is not the plan that is magical. The magic is in executing the plan. However, in order to execute a plan, you do need to start with a plan. It is important you convey your plan to everyone in the program and turn it from "your" plan to "our" plan. You are better off to have people working together on an average plan than to have no plan at all. It does not matter if you like to do things different than we did them in our program: Just have a plan!

Here are the important factors:
- ✓ Write it down
- ✓ Be clear, concise, and realistic
- ✓ Make "your" plan into "our" plan
- ✓ Execute your plan

Write it down

We had a plan for everything and as much as possible it was written down. You can use PowerPoint, manuals, or whatever method you prefer but I learned you need to have a written plan for as many things as possible. If you are not a great word processor, find someone that can help you and dictate to them what you want. I cannot stress enough how important it is to write down your vision and plan for every aspect of your program. This process makes you reflect and teaches the author as much as the reader. Many of the things I learned as a leader I learned having to put my thoughts down into paper.

Try to think of as many little things as possible when you are documenting your plans. You need to understand you will never think of everything, but the more things you think of the better the plan will be. You must execute and implement this plan so the more detail, the better. You will never remember as many details as you think so it is best to write them down when they are fresh, so you have them as a reference later.

A key to writing a successful plan is to begin with the end in mind. Think about where you want to end up and work backwards on how you are going to get there. Think of a "plan" as another word for a "vision". You must have a vision for your program and this vision should be written down. This can be a tedious and difficult process and this is why most people do not have all their ideas documented. Get over it being difficult. If it were easy, everyone would do it.

Your written plan needs to include answers to the following:

- ❖ What is our plan to reward and award people in our program?
- ❖ What is our social media plan? How can we get more organized with it?
- ❖ What is our plan to work with the other sports and groups in the school?
- ❖ What is our plan to make it fun?
- ❖ What team building activities will we do? How can we make them meaningful?
- ❖ What is our scheme? This can be different by sport but put your scheme on paper.
- ❖ What is our plan for strength and conditioning?
- ❖ What is our plan to develop players on our sub-varsity teams?
- ❖ What are our booster club plan and procedures?
- ❖ What are our procedures for dealing with parents?
- ❖ What is our plan to develop our coaching staff?
- ❖ What is our plan to periodically evaluate our program?
- ❖ What is our plan for player discipline and policies?
- ❖ What is our plan for practice? Be precise and cover little things. Make sure everyone (coach and player) always knows where to be.
- ❖ What is our plan for games? Be precise and cover little things. Make sure everyone (coach and player) always knows where to be.

<u>Write it down: How do you do it?</u>

- ✓ **Begin with the end in mind** – think about where you want to be in the future and write down how you are doing to get there

- ✓ **Little things** – leave no stone unturned; think of as many things as possible before they happen and add them to your plan

- ✓ **Get over it being hard** – it is supposed to be hard; if it were easy, everyone would do it!

Be clear, concise, and realistic

Many people seek the title "hardest working" at their job. I have learned to seek to be the most efficient and effective person at your job. Sometimes the hardest working person is not the most successful person or the person that accomplishes the most. Obviously, you must have a great work ethic to be successful, but you should strive to be effective and efficient. Efficiency starts in being clear, concise, and realistic in your plan building.

Many people assume way too much when they are developing their plan. You should give clear and concise roles to each person in your organization and have clear and concise expectations and plans. You must communicate your vision. You will likely have to say it over and over and produce it in many forms. The excuse of "I told them…." is not good enough if you want to be successful. It does not matter what you "told" them; it matters what they "understand". Giving clear expectations is great because it saves time in the long run. Effective work should always be the measuring stick more than length of work.

Be logical in your approach. Have a realistic plan that you can execute. Having "pie in the sky" plans can make the entire plan difficult to execute. If you are unrealistic in your approach, the realistic parts of your plan will not be as successful because it will seem inefficient and ineffective. A great example of being logical comes with building a scheme for your team. Since I coached football, I will give a football analogy. If we are planning our offense and we know that the average game for 10 years has been 60 offensive plays, we do not need to carry combinations of 500+ plays into the game. (Yes, people do this). You will need plays for all situations and hashes but that is it. You practice those plays and make it work. Of course, it would be better if you could run everything and run them all out of every formation, but that is not realistic or logical. Another example would be giving a coach something to do in the job responsibilities that they can not do. That is not logical. Make sure you are giving them jobs that they can perform successfully.

Unfortunately, one of the main ways to do this is through "trial and error". Therefore, it is so important to take notes after events and evaluate yourself. We evaluated ourselves on everything. After the evaluation we would change the plan for next time so that when it came around again, we were more prepared. This is particularly true with fundraisers, parent meetings, and banquets. Make notes after the event is over on what you would have done differently and then change your written plan. This way it will be more effective and efficient the next time around. How many times have you seen people say, "next year we need to...." only to make the exact same mistake next year because they forgot. I have seen this happen many times. Get organized and come up with a system to make notes and change things as you find better, more effective ways to accomplish the goal.

Be clear, concise, and realistic: How do you do it?

- ✓ **Effectiveness over length** – work smart and be organized so you can maximize your time. Judge the success of your plan by how effective it was and not the length of time each person is working. They do not give out extra points to start the game for winning "longest time in the field house"

- ✓ **Be logical in your approach** – find realistic, logical things when making your plan. Make sure these are things you can do and get accomplished.

✓ **Make notes** – come up with a system on how to self-evaluate. Make notes when things are less effective than you thought they would be and make the necessary corrections the next time around. Do not get caught in the cycle of unprepared.

Make "your" plan into "our" plan

So, you created a plan and put it into writing. You worked to make that plan as concise and clear as it could be. It is "your" plan. You now need to turn it into "our" plan. When your plan becomes our plan, the magic will start happening. It is a great feeling to see the plan begin to work and you can see the excitement in the athletes, coaches, parents, and administration. Taking your plan and turning into our plan means you have convinced people that they now share the same vision as you. This is much easier said than done. It involves respect, trust, and many other intangibles. This is where building the relationships we talked about in the first lesson become so crucial.

I do not believe anyone in leadership wants to appear selfish or self-serving, but many people do. There are a few things you can do to help you look more like the humble, team player you aspire to be. Being good at these things has a lot to do with getting others to believe in your vision. Remember, by someone believing in your vision, they are believing in YOU. This is a powerful thing that is not taken lightly and not easily attainable. Again, remember half the teams lose all contest. It is hard to win!

One of the first methods to show everyone that although you are the leader, it is "our" program is proper use of pronouns. I can not stand people saying things like "my players", "my coaches", "my field", etc. I would always say "our players", "our coaches", "our field". I did not own anything. I was the leader of the ship but all people on the ship were important! This is a common mistake that most do not do deliberately but there is an issue with these pronouns. People are subconsciously turned off by those that make everything possessive. Make sure you include words like "we", "us", "our" as much as possible.

Another key component of getting your vision to become the program's vision is to be a good listener. Sometimes we all "wait to talk" instead of genuinely listening to the other person. I am working on doing better at this myself. Dr. Charles Webb is the best listener I have ever been around. Dr. Webb was only an interim supervisor of mine but in a short time I grew to respect him as much as anyone. He was a long-time Head Football Coach, Athletic Director, Principal, and Superintendent in South Georgia. He also served as a General in the National Guard. He had an amazing career. When he came to North Georgia to serve as interim superintendent, he knew he would not be there long, and he knew no one had a resume near his. I was blown away at how intently he would listen to everyone talk. He would remember things that you told him weeks earlier. He never interrupted and he allowed others to speak. This made everyone feel like he cared and whatever plan or vision he had for our department, we wanted to make our plan. Listening is a powerful tool.

You also need to be good at mixing plans. Find every opportunity to tie your plan to something someone else suggested or wants to do. If you wanted to have a car wash but one of the parents, assistant coaches, or others came to you and said they wanted to do a car wash, do not tell them "I was already planning on doing that". Instead, tell them "that's a great idea! Let's do it!". The approach is so important. They came to you with a proposal and you do not have to feel the need to let them know that you "thought of it first". Include people in the decisions and planning process. If they can tweak it slightly from your original plan but it is better, that is fantastic. If it is not something you want to do, you can omit it from the plan, but they will know you listened to some of the other ideas and they will respect your decisions.

Make your plan into our plan: How do you do it?

✓ **Pronouns matter** – Try to avoid using words "I", "my", etc. when describing the program. Say "we", "our", "us" instead. We are all in this together. People are subconsciously turned off by possessive words in a group effort.

✓ **Be a good listener** – you always hear the phrase "you have 2 ears and 1 mouth for a reason". Listen to people and show you genuinely value what they are saying. Listening will help you earn respect.

✓ **Mix plans** – mix your plan with what others suggest whenever possible. Your plan can be the final authority but do not feel the need to take away any input of value in the opinion of others.

Execute the plan

As mentioned earlier, a good plan is worth nothing if not executed. You will be excited about your plan as you are compiling it. You will gain confidence and feel like this plan will help you succeed. As you start implementation, something will derail your plan. Something always derails the plan. It could be something you forgot to think about, or it could be something beyond your control. Regardless of the reason, rest assured your plan will be difficult to execute. This is the reason it is so special when you make it happen!

One of the keys to executing your plans is to work to not let your feelings get in the way. In my experience, hurt feelings are often the thief of good plans. A person will have a good plan, but when the administration makes a change or a player gets in trouble, the person that worked so hard at the plan loses focus and either alters the course or gives up. Your vision should steer your decisions and not your feelings. We have a whole "lesson" dedicated to that later! Execute your plan regardless of the hurdles that are thrown in front of you. One of the best ways to do this is to be prepared. Accept that there WILL be hurdles to your plan, and it will be difficult to execute. Keep the program's vision in the front of your mind. Then when something bad happens, you just adapt and move on. You can be disappointed that something went wrong, but you can not let it affect the next decision. We always told our players the most important play was "the next play". As a leader, the most important decision is always "the next decision". Remember what has happened is over and all you can control is your attitude and effort moving forward.

Another concept to remember when executing your plan is that the plan can change. I struggled with this at times. I worked on a plan and I would get frustrated when it had to change. I became a much better coach when I realized it was inevitable that it would change, and I just changed with it. Constantly evolve and adapt your plan. Some ideas work at one place that may not work at another place. If you said you hated something but now want to do it, so what? It is alright for you to change your mind, change your vision, and change your plan. The key to the plan is the constant evaluation and execution. Keep in mind you do not have to have the "perfect" plan, you just need a plan and you need to keep improving it.

You need to be accountable to your plan and own it. When it needs to change, do not hesitate to change it, and move on. This is a career-long pursuit for the "perfect" plan. You will never get there, but you will come up with some great plans along the way. If you have struggled many times before, keep going. You have just not succeeded "yet". Keep in mind that you never fail until you quit. Never, ever, ever quit working on your vision and your plan. It is always a "work in progress".

Executing the plan: How do you do it?

- ✓ **Do not get your feelings hurt** – keep the vision of the program at the front and do not be derailed by frustration.

- ✓ **Execute plan regardless of hurdles** – there will be hurdles. Accept that now and be ready to adapt when they come.

- ✓ **Be adaptable – your plan can change** – it is acceptable to change your stance on things as you evolve as a leader. Do not let stubbornness supersede your desire to win!

✓ **Be accountable** – own your plan; have confidence it will work but be flexible when you need to change it. Have a method to evaluate your plan periodically.

✓ **Never quit working on your vision and plan** – your plan only fails when you quit. If it has not succeeded "yet", keep adapting and keep working!

Conclusion

Coming up with a plan is a great way to improve your program. Learning how to execute that plan is an even better way. Putting plans together can be tedious and exhausting, but it is worth it. You need to start with a vision, in writing, of where your program stands at that moment.

All the "lessons" in this book help you execute your plan. The next chapter focuses on one of the most important aspects in executing your plan: Communication.

Lesson Three:

Over-Communicate

People that know me might say I am an "over-communicator" if there is such a thing! I like to talk to people and I like emails. If I have information that I need to get out I like to post things on multiple social media platforms, email, text, etc. If you were in our program, I hoped I was giving you too much information as opposed to not enough. Communication is a key to any program's success.

Several good things happen when you are a good communicator. People trust you have a plan and give you the benefit of the doubt when there is some confusion. There will always be breakdowns in communication but if you are a good communicator, you will not suffer the ill effects of lack of communication. Effective communication is enormously powerful and comes in many forms. Communication can be formal or informal, direct or electronic. Regardless of the type of communication, it must be effective.

Being a good communicator will solve most problems before they arise. If you are a good communicator, you are not even aware of the number of things that you never had to deal with, so it is hard to quantify how much time it saves. You never had to deal with that confused or frustrated parent that did not realize what time practice ended because details were communicated. If you do not believe this, let someone less successful at communicating attempt to do the same job and notice how many more conversations the administration is having with parents.

Everyone can be a better communicator. Strive to find ways to get your message and vision relayed to everyone in your program better than the year before. Here are some ways you can be a better communicator:

Here are the important factors:
- ✓ Embrace the new thing
- ✓ Cover it electronically
- ✓ Directly communicate
- ✓ Organization

Embrace the new thing

When I was starting out in coaching, older coaches loved to tell the stories of the 16mm film and driving hours to get it developed. Coaches my age love to talk about making cutups on VHS tapes and having to go meet the other team to exchange videos at random places and times. Those "back in the day" stories are great but if you are not embracing the new thing, you are getting behind. This is true in all ten "Lessons" but it is most true with communication. When I started coaching, the internet was just getting big and it was a big deal if your team had a website and a newsletter. Now social media is the tool. Social media is great marketing and it is great at communicating. I have no doubt one of the reasons we were successful at growing our programs was embracing social media. Some people were late to embrace this new thing and it has cost them.

One of the many reasons for any success I had was my younger brother, Michael. Michael and I worked together basically my entire career. I ran the Offense and was the Head Coach while Michael ran the Defense. Michael and I worked great together. I knew I always had someone that was loyal and was pushing in the same direction as me. When we first moved to Pickens, Michael approached me about social media. He said we need to have a team Facebook and Twitter. I knew what Facebook was, but I did not have a personal Facebook. I had no real idea what Twitter was. I think I said something like, "we don't need all that". He kept pushing and finally made one anyway and he managed it. I did not pay much attention to it for a few months but then I started realizing how engaged people were to what we posted. We had gone to coaching clinics and recruiting expos for years but when we posted a picture of us at the event people were so happy and proud that we were promoting our players or growing our crafts. We were not doing anything differently; we were just advertising it better. I realize now this may seem commonplace, but back then very few coaches were doing this. It gave us a great method to communicate to our community. Before long, I was taking over the "Pickens Football" Twitter and Facebook and posting even more often than Michael.

Social Media is great, but you should not depend on this alone. If we were cancelling practice, I wanted to let everyone know. Social Media was a good start, but we would also email, use texting apps like Remind 101, and make announcements at school (like the "old" days!). It is your job as the leader of the program to communicate and meet them where they are – not the other way around. Do not put something out there "to say you did it". Put the message out there wherever and however it can be received by everyone.

Embracing the new thing can be challenging. I do not always embrace it in my personal life. I enjoy doing things the way I like to do them but as a coach, it is your job to maximize potential. If there is a new way to do anything, you should at least investigate it and ask yourself, "is this something that can help our program grow?" If you do not have a younger brother that coaches with you and lets you know the new things, you can talk to your players and parents. Ask them what the best way is to communicate with them. Be humble and let them know you only care about getting the message out, you are not concerned with how you do it. Whatever works best for them should work best for you.

The moral of the story: For one of the very few times ever, Michael was right, and I was wrong! Social media was a great addition to our program. Social media will be old news one day and there will be something else. Embrace the new thing!

Embrace the new thing: How do you do it?

- ✓ **Do not be scared to get out of your comfort zone** – find people who will share with you new ideas and ways to communicate

- ✓ **Talk to player and parents** – ask them how they would like for you to communicate; Meet them where they are

✓ **Keep your eyes and ears open** – Do not assume there is not a new thing coming that you have never thought of yet!

Cover it Electronically

Being a good communicator makes the program run so much smoother because people understand their roles and the expectations. One of the reasons I loved communicating via email was I could document covering my bases and go back and verify what I said. This is useful when self-evaluating the plan or when you must correct someone for not doing their part. Taking your plan and communicating it to all stakeholders will be essential in your program's success. As an Athletic Director, the most common complaints I heard from people about coaches was "they do not communicate" or "no one let us know". Whether this was true or not, it is a standard argument parents make about coaches. Everyone can communicate better. You must be a good communicator to cover yourself.

➢ **Cover it with other Players**: Players now know nothing but electronic communication. There are plenty of Apps and groups out there that allow you to communicate with the team. Find one that works for you and use it. Never give them the excuse of "no one told me!" Communicate your expectations for the program. We did this in a player's manual that included procedures, policies and our character education program.   We also signed players up for communication apps and we made sure we had everyone's contact information.

> **Cover it with Coaches:** Send the coaches exactly what you need from them. I emailed coaches daily practice plans and responsibilities during the season. I know they got tired of me sending out plans, but I would rather have them tired of that than being confused of what to do. Occasionally I had to remind one of them of their job with the phrase, "it was in the email I sent out today". Communicating electronically also should make for shorter meetings. It is important to respect the assistant coach's time. They do not make the money the head coach makes, and they are not usually in positions to complain. It is your job as the leader to respect their time. One of the best ways to respect their time is email them everything that can be communicated that way to shorten the meetings.

> **Cover it with Parents:** Let parents know of your expectations and ways they can participate. Try not to wait until they ask. You may not be able to control if they participate or confirm to your expectations but you can make sure no one says they did not realize we needed their participation or no one sent them the expectations, calendar, etc. Parents will say, "I will do whatever you want, I just need someone to let me know." I am not sure they always mean that, but if you communicate well you at least cover that excuse.

> ➤ **Cover it with Admin:** Always send your annual calendar, responsibilities, and other documentation to you send out to the Administration. It is likely they will not care one way or the other, but it shows you have a plan and you are sending them what you are doing. I always sent the principal all our coaching responsibilities and calendars. They did not always look at them, but they knew they had access. I felt like it was better to send this information to them before they needed to ask for it.

> ➤ **Cover it with other leaders:** Make sure you are documenting your conversations with the leaders of the other sports, band directors, etc. You are not doing this to "get" them but to make sure you have communicated properly. It is always a good idea to send too much rather than not enough. I would try to send the cheer and band leaders as many things as possible that we were sending to coaches, players, and parents. They probably did not care anything about getting all this documentation, but they could not say they were not informed. The same goes for working calendars for players that play multiple sports. Making clear plans that are communicated electronically will eliminate most of the problems before they ever arise.

Cover it: How do you do it?

> ✓ **Emails** – emails are a great way to document and to share information without having to have a meeting. Use them as much as possible. Have a system yourself to check and reply to emails. Make it a priority to get back to people as soon as you can when they email you.

✓ **Create calendars and share with all stakeholders** – calendars or player manuals are not top-secret information. Send them to admin, other sports' coaches, parents, etc. Find a way to get it to everyone involved.

✓ **Website/Social media** – put as many things as you can on your team sites so you can always reference people back to the site to find the information.

Directly Communicate

As important as it is to document things and have written plans, nothing will be more effective than direct communication. This is becoming a lost art. From the time I started coaching through today, the thing that has changed the most with players is their inability to communicate directly. They would much rather text or send you a message electronically than they would talk to you. That is why you MUST talk to them. You must develop that relationship with them so you can directly communicate with them. This should be done formally and informally. Three different ways to directly communicate should can be used:

1. **Formal:** You can set up times to talk to people. Have meetings and plan the agenda of what you will discuss. Talk about their goals and aspirations and how together you can get there.

2. **"Informal":** This is where you make yourself a note or list of people to directly communicate with, but it appears informal. You find a way to talk to them and

ask how they are doing and talk some about your vision for them in the program.

3. **Impromptu:** These are not planned at all. When the situation presents itself, you must take advantage of an opportunity to directly communicate with people in the program and share your vision for them.

Use formal, informal, and impromptu methods to directly communicate your vision for the entire program and your vision for each individual person. There is great power in direct communication. It is a power that is growing stronger by the year as it is becoming a rare trait. If you are a young, aspiring coach I challenge you to force yourself to directly communicate. Occasionally talk to someone when it would be easier to text them. Make yourself have some direct conversations with people. If you become a good direct communicator, you will separate yourself from your peers in your ability to lead.

Directly communicating with Players

With anything involving coaching, the players are the most important group. They will not be great at directly communicating back to you. You will have to "carry the load" at first.

➢ **Formal:** Twice a year, I sat down with each player in our program and talked to them for 5-10 minutes. We would discuss goals and vision for them, and our plans moving forward. I would always talk to each player on the team about where they stood and how they could improve. I would listen and answer any questions they had. You would think it is no big deal to talk for 5-10 minutes, but when you have over 100 players, it took me weeks to get it completed. We accomplished so many things preemptively doing this. I think this was one of the more powerful things we did.

> **Informal:** At least twice a year I made sure that I "bumped" into our players in the school and had a conversation with them. I would print off a roster and cross off people as I talked to them. I wanted to see them in the cafeteria, hallways, basketball games, etc. Most coaches talk to their players in this way, but I wanted to make sure I did not miss anyone, so I kept up with it. I was going to make sure each student had at least a few conversations with me during the year, away from the field.

> **Impromptu:** The unplanned meetings with the players are some of the best. You must seize the opportunity when they want to talk and continue to share your vision for them and the team. If you have to talk to a player about something else, slip in a conversation about things they are doing well and things they can work on.

Directly communicating with Assistant Coaches

Communication with the coaches is the communication that is most likely to help with organization and efficiency. Coaches need to believe in the leader and share the same vision. Directly communicating with them will be the best way to share your vision for the program.

➢ **Formal:** Obviously, there are group coaching meetings scheduled often. These are not the things addressed here. Direct communication with the coaches involves sitting down with them individually and talking to them about their career plans, things they do well, and things to improve upon. This usually happens at the end of the season. Some coaches struggle to sit down and have these conversations. Make it a point to set a schedule to meet with each coach after the season for a formal meeting.

➢ **Informal:** These can be the most powerful meetings with coaches. Attempt to prevent discontent and apathy by making a point to talk to each coach individually throughout the year about how things are going. This can be done on the field, in the school setting, or in a social setting. Let them know they are supported. Division on the coaching staff is one of the quickest ways for your program to deteriorate.

➢ **Impromptu:** As a Head Coach, when an assistant coach needs to talk to you, it is usually about another job, wanting a title, or some other personal issue. Regardless if you can or cannot accommodate their request, it provides a great platform to talk about your vision and share ways we can all get better. Sometimes they may present good points that can change your vision as well.

Directly communicating with Parents

Being proactive and preemptive in parent communication will save you time and headaches. While most communication with parents will be electronically, it is important to have successful direct communication with parents.

> **Formal:** Group parent meetings are a great way to sell your vision. I preferred to do them by grade level so the groups would be smaller. This seemed more effective. I would not meet with parents individually on a schedule like we did with coaches and parents, but I would meet with parents when they requested it. I did not discuss playing time, scheme, or other people's children. If the topics did not include those three things, I was happy to meet formally with a parent anytime. It is important when meeting with a parent in a formal meeting that you show them respect. Try to see the issue from their point of view as much as possible.

> **Informal & Impromptu:** For parents, there is not a distinct difference between informal and impromptu. The main way these occur is when you see a parent out at a baseball game, the grocery store, etc. I would always make a point to speak to them. Do not avoid them. Be friendly and let them see you as a human being. I tried to keep the talk as light as possible and always ask how their child was doing. Sometimes just bumping into someone and appearing to care is a powerful thing.

Directly communicating with Administration

Administration has a great impact on the success of any program but that "administrative support" that all coaches strive for is earned. You need to be a good communicator with your administration. Some of this needs to be direct.

> **Formal:** Set up at least one meeting a year (preferably two) where you ask the administration what you are doing well, what you can work on, and what is their vision for the future of your program. Many positive conversations can result from you taking the initiative and setting up these meetings. Do not wait for them to call you. Make an agenda and have specific questions and topics for the meeting.

> **Informal & Impromptu:** When you happen to run into the administration on or off campus, make a point to speak and be positive. Do not be someone who only brings up negative things. Take these moments to brag on your program. Say something like, "I've been meaning to tell you about…." and make it something positive most of the time. You will find that your administrative support will grow.

Directly communicating with other groups

You can correct so many issues before they ever happen by being a good communicator with other sports/groups in the school.

> **Formal:** Set an annual time for you to sit down with each coach/sponsor that works directly with your program and ask them what you are doing well, what you can work on and talk about the vision for both programs moving forward.

> **Informal:** Make it a point to attend events when possible and support those teams. When you do find the coach/sponsor, make sure to tell them "good luck" or

"congratulations" or whatever would be appropriate at that time.

➢ **Impromptu:** When situations present themselves for you to have to talk to the leaders of other organizations in your school, make the most of it. Try to talk to them about your vision and how both programs can grow by working together.

Directly communicate: How do you do it?

✓ **Set up formal meetings** – find time and plan individual and group meetings. You can even set the schedule for the entire year. The challenge is to stick to the meetings. It is difficult to take this much time, and it will feel like "more important" things will take you away, but this is worth the time and is important!

✓ **Set up formal, informal meetings** – find times to talk to the people in your program informally. Even if you must make a list to make sure you see everyone, you should prioritize to take advantage of this powerful tool.

✓ **Take advantage of the impromptu opportunities** – when opportunity presents itself, sit down and talk to the people in your program about your vision and their goals and how they can align.

Organization

"Get organized" is one of the most trivial things people say when giving advice. Obviously, being organized is better than not being organized, but I have never met anyone that did not want to be organized. We need an understanding of how to get organized. When it pertains to communication, organization means finding processes that allow you to be a better communicator. Plan times to communicate with all the people in the program. You can set formal meetings and even schedule times of the year to have informal discussions with people in the program. Set these meetings up by the method that best fits your style. Put them on your calendar and stick to the schedule. It will be hard to have so many meetings, but they will be helpful, useful, and effective.

Go ahead and admit to yourself that you are not perfect. You are going to forget things. Set a reminder in your phone to "tell parents about equipment pick up", "remind about booster club meeting", etc. This is the biggest part of getting organized. When communication breaks down it is rarely because it was intentional; someone just forgot. The fewer times you forget, the better. Do not just assume you will remember to communicate. Use the most updated technology to help you remember. We have great tools now at our disposal to help us get organized. Your program needs you to utilize them!

Have a standard agenda for most meetings. For more formal, annual meetings with coaches I liked to send out a google form survey that allowed the coach to answer the key questions about the meeting and submit it before. I found this effective as the coach could think of the answers to questions like, "what are we doing well", "what do we need to improve on", "where do you see yourself in 5 years" with time to reflect and answer. I would use those answers with the standard agenda to have a plan for each individual meeting.

Take notes during meetings and make sure you transfer those notes to your "to do" list or, if necessary, to the written plans you have. This can be a key step that is commonly omitted. Imagine you are in a meeting with an assistant coach, and you are talking about something they need. You tell them you will investigate it and get back to them. Then you never do. This is a breakdown of communication that could hurt your relationship. If you get back to that coach soon and have an answer, they know you care about them enough to investigate something for them and follow up. In meetings, we are often full of good ideas that do not go anywhere. Make sure you follow up on all things discussed in the meeting.

Once you have a plan in place, organization can also be called "consistency". Sometimes people are motivated for a short period of time to get more organized and communicate better. Over time, distractions or frustration makes it difficult to continue with the plan. Organization takes discipline but it will make you a better communicator. Make communication a priority.

Organization: How do you do it?

- ✓ **Set reminders** – use the best available technology to keep yourself organized on communicating with all members of your team. These can be set weeks or even months in advance.

- ✓ **Send surveys/evaluations** – send people surveys or evaluations at least annually. Gather the information and use it to make your program better.

- ✓ **Have an agenda/outline** – have a standard agenda for each formal meeting (player, coach, admin, etc.) Adjust the standard agenda based on the individual situation and answers from the survey, if applicable, to create a unique agenda for that meeting. Make sure all meetings have a purpose.

- ✓ **Make notes** – Take notes in meetings and then transfer those notes to your reminders or manuals to make sure the good ideas of your meeting are not lost. Follow up on all things you said you would do in the meeting.

- ✓ **Consistency** – even when it gets hard or you are discouraged, stick to your plan to communicate. Stay on schedule!

Conclusion

Being a better communicator is essential to self-growth. If you want the program to grow under your leadership, you must be an effective communicator. Find ways that fit your personal style and methods to be a better communicator. Use paper and pencil, smartphones, and everything in between that fits your style to get yourself more organized and be a better communicator. Like most things in life, communication takes discipline, organization, and hard work.

Once you have a grasp on the importance of communication, you can move on to another key component of successful leadership: presentation and delivery.

Lesson Four:

It's all in the presentation

Once you have a great plan, and great methods to communicate your message, you must master presenting and delivering the information. Your message can take off or be ruined in how you present and deliver the information. You can make people believe in you, or doubt you, based on the presentation. While it is important to have a plan and communicate your plan, the skills you use to communicate will have everything to do with how the information is received and processed. It is easier said than done to get people to clearly understand the message you are attempting to deliver.

My wife, Kimberly, has taught me many things over the years. We are raising two girls together, and one of the many things I have learned from Kimberly is that presentation matters. When our daughters were young, I learned that you must present information properly to get your desired result. If you ask a toddler if they want to take a bath, they may say "no" and scream. If you ask them if they want to take a bath or go ahead and get ready for bed, they are running to the bathtub. It was all in the presentation!

The message is important, but the delivery of the message will determine how the message is received. When you are a good presenter you can better share your vision. People want to follow those who can clearly show their vision. When you can put something in the proper context and make your point, you will be much more effective as a leader. I recognize some people are better presenters than others, but there are things you can do to make yourself a good presenter. Selling the program is a big part of being a successful leader and it is not an excuse to say, "I'm not good at that". If you like to succeed, you must get good at it. Work on this craft and use the important factors that are laid out to make yourself the best presenter you can be.

Here are some examples of times when presentation and delivery matter most

➢ *Coming up with a new thing to do for your team this year* – how did you present that to the team? You need to make this appear like the greatest thing on Earth and you must make it a big deal if you want them to make it a big deal.

➤ *Dealing with discipline* – let the players know that you are not punishing them out of anger but out of love. Let them know the punishment is designed to help them and grow them into a better person and athlete. You have to show them you care about them, you just cannot accept this behavior.

➤ *Dealing with parents* – you must make the parents feel like you have it under control. Show that you understand their point of view, give them any ownership you can give them, but let them know you have the vision to grow the program. With parents, they are not going to do it "because you said so", you have to make them "want" to do it.

➤ *Fundraising* – I have found that fundraising is a place where presentation and delivery can be everything. You need people to be "sold" on what you are literally selling AND what vision you have for their money.

➤ *Dealing with administration* – do not spend their time talking about things neither of you can control. Present realistic visions and plans to reach common goals. The administration is so busy they will not respect anyone wasting their time.

➤ *Dealing with recruiting* – show the prospective student-athletes and their parents that you know what you are talking about. If you have information from college coaches directly or connections, use them. Learn the process so you can genuinely present yourself as someone familiar with the process.

Here are the important factors:
- ✓ Preparation
- ✓ Think outside the box
- ✓ Confidence
- ✓ Speak it into existence

Preparation

Presentation and delivery can occur in one-on-one meetings or in large group meetings. While one is more formal than the other, there is not a distinction between one being more important. You must be able to deliver information to large groups when necessary and you must be able to talk to small groups or even one individual, and present information in a way all audiences can understand. Like almost everything else, the best way to assure success in your presentation is to be prepared.

Organizing your thoughts is the most obvious way to prepare. Preparation does not mean you must create an elaborate "presentation"; it just means you need to be prepared for the meetings. Keeping up a calendar is easier than it has ever been, and you should know your planned meetings for the day. Take a few moments each morning to think about what you are doing with each meeting and maybe even take a few notes to make sure you are prepared. Think about what you want to say and what you hope to get accomplished. Think about ways you can relate the message to your audience, like using an old story or metaphor. Anything you can think of ahead of time will make the likelihood of success much higher.

Do not start a planned meeting with that moment being the first time you have thought about the subject. This is a how a great message gets lost with poor presentation. I hate hearing people say, "I'm good at winging it." Nobody is good at that. It just means you settled for less than your best. Think about what you are going to say and then, if necessary, give the same talk to yourself. When I was starting out as an Assistant football coach, I taught U.S. History at Sequoyah High School. There was no coincidence that I was much better at the discussion in 3rd period than I was 1st period. The more times you deliver the message, the better you will be.

The key is to look like you are "winging it" when it is actually well thought out. These are the best presentations. No one wants a robotic, boring presentation. But a presentation that has had little preparation will not be as effective as it could have been, regardless of the talent of the presenter. This is especially true in your coaching meetings. Present to them that you are organized but also flexible enough to be approachable.

If you are planning a large gathering like a parent meeting or banquet, you must do a great job of preparation for the event. Remember, you are the leader of the program so you should act like it. Parents will respect someone that has an organized presentation. Bring your "A" game with the large gatherings so that you can maximize the effects of the event.

Unplanned meetings are obviously impossible to directly prepare for, but if you have a real grasp of presenting you can still use these opportunities to share your vision. Use the databank of metaphors and stories in your head when needing to present information to someone "on the fly". As a leader, it is important to have this database ready. Always make sure you are as prepared as you can be when you present and deliver information.

Preparation: How do you do it?

- ✓ **Organize your thoughts** – review daily what you must do and how you can best present the information necessary.

- ✓ **Never present unprepared** – it is lazy and not your best. Even if you are a good natural speaker, work to be even better by practicing and thinking about what you are going to say.

Think outside the box

My friend, Dr. Chad Flatt, has said that I have a unique ability to tell people something they do not want to hear and make them like it. I do not know if that is true or not, but I assume he is giving me a compliment! Chad was a Head Football Coach and came to work with me as an Offensive Line Coach when I was the Head Coach at Chapel Hill. He then came to Pickens High with me, and he and I have become great friends. Coach Flatt quickly became Dr. Flatt, was hired as an assistant principal, and later a principal. Chad and I are the same age and have grown as leaders together. We always talk about the value of presentation and how the message is delivered. He has been a good leader in all his roles. We are always trying to do a better job of presenting our information. When Chad became the first ever principal of the newly created Pickens Junior High School, he immediately began a campaign to present and deliver information in the best ways possible. This is an undervalued trait among all types of leaders. One of the many things that Chad taught me was how to create an App. He saw a presentation at a conference and told me about it. We took this idea and have created Apps for his school, athletic department, and now for all employees in our district. We had to think outside of the box to help deliver our information.

Do not go through the motions and just do what has always been done. Explore what other people are doing and expand on that. Chad had the idea from the App, I helped expand on that idea. This is true partnership. The worst phrase in the English language may be, "that's what we have always done." Be an innovator and a pioneer. Have a vision for what you want and work backwards from there to help achieve it. Research as many ways as possible to do things and then think of new things that stem from those ideas.

Anytime you are trying new things, you may fail. You must get over the fear of failure if you want to truly succeed. I have had many good ideas over the years that helped our program grow, but I have had many bad ideas that we tried and then scrapped. You must be willing to go out on a limb for your program and try new things. This can be the best way to expand your program and present it in a light that is more favorable than before.

Many of my best ideas came from someone else and then I expanded upon it. There are plenty of great programs out there that you can research and study. Analyze them and think outside the box to come up with new ideas to make your program better.

Think outside the box: How do you do it?

- ✓ **Try new things** – do not think you know everything, and your way is perfect. Always look at new ways to present your program and deliver information.

- ✓ **Eliminate "that's how we have always done it"** – evaluate every aspect of the program and understand why you do it. If you have no answer other than this, get rid of it.

✓ **Do not be scared to fail** – you will fail sometimes when you are thinking outside the box. Failure in one idea is just one step closer to the great idea!

Confidence

Confidence is really a key in successful presentation and delivery. You must sell these people on you and make them believe you are the person who can bring them further than they have ever gone. There is no way to do this if you do not believe it yourself. Humans pick up on the following traits inherently and quickly: confident, charismatic, engaging, nervous, timid, scared. While three of these are good for presentation and three are not, it is important to understand that these are the traits to know. Work at showing the three positive traits and avoiding the negatives. Make sure you come across as confident by actually believing in yourself! Someone gave you the job you have because they believed in you. Work hard to prove them right! Tell yourself, "I got this" and go make it happen.

Anyone that has spent some time in the North Georgia Mountains knows that Pickens County and Gilmer County are rivals. They compete in everything. The story goes that Pickens stayed loyal to the Union in the Civil War and Gilmer supported the Confederacy. The disdain carried onto the gridiron. When I got to Pickens, they had lost to the rival

Bobcats several years in a row. Gilmer did have an incredibly talented, well-coached team, but I was certain we would beat them in my first year at Pickens. Unfortunately, my confidence was not relayed to the majority. We did not beat them as they just played harder than us and our team had no confidence that we would win the game.

It perplexed me that we struggled so much against a team that was a lot like us. Our Assistant Head Coach at Pickens, Sam Wigington, and I are great friends and we have always discussed everything involving the football program. We talked all off-season about ways we could be more confident. This is about the time I started realizing that it did not matter what I wanted to do to help us win, it mattered what the players wanted to do. The players wanted to wear black. The uniforms were green, white, black, and gray over the years at Pickens, but we had no black in the uniform at that time. I told them in 2014 we would get black helmets. The players were so excited. It was interesting to me to see the level of excitement for a color. As we were preparing to get ready to buy uniforms that year, Sam and I cooked up a scheme: We would buy these black jerseys, tell no one about them, and break them out the day of the Gilmer game. We had already decided I would exude more confidence against Gilmer and that would trickle down to the players.

On Halloween 2014 we were set to play Gilmer. Both teams entered the game 7-1. Playoff positioning and possible region championship implications were on the line. The game was at our stadium. Pickens had not beaten Gilmer in years. I spent all week showing clips from the Bad Boys Detroit Pistons teams, specifically how they beat up the Chicago Bulls led by Michael Jordan. Finally, by Thursday, I showed the Bulls dominate the Pistons in 1991 and the Pistons walking off the court without even shaking their hands. I made a big deal about how we had to "take the game to them" and quit getting pushed around. We had to quit being afraid of messing up and seize this opportunity. We had a great week of practice. The guys were ready to play.

We went to warmup like always and the stadium was packed. There was always a great crowd at the Gilmer game, but with both teams having such a good season, it was special. We had our regular green jerseys on, and the players were ready to go. Sam had coordinated that day to get a couple of coaches involved in our plan. These coaches got their black jerseys thrown in the player's locker during warmups. When those players came back to the locker room after warmups, I have never seen a group of guys more fired up. I think at some point in the year they asked about black jerseys and I went on a rant about how jersey colors do not matter. They had no idea this was coming. We had the PA announcer play "Back in

Black" by AC/DC as we came down the hill to the game. The entire place went crazy.

I have no idea if those jerseys helped but I do know we caused a fumble on the 3rd play, scored 2 plays later, and won the game 42-19. I do believe the confidence that we were able to show that entire week was felt by our players and they played confidently. We had to show the players we were planning on winning before we could win. I coached in four more Pickens-Gilmer games after that Halloween game in 2014, and we won all of them!

Confidence: How do you do it?

- ✓ **Believe in yourself** – no one is going to believe in you if you do not believe in yourself. You need to have a positive attitude and make sure you are genuinely confident you can succeed.

- ✓ **Fake it until you make it** – even if you are not always sure, always show confidence and let the people in the program feel like we have the plan that is going to help them succeed.

- ✓ **Find ways to show you believe in people** – it may take many different methods but find a way to show the people in your program they can believe in you and you believe in them.

Speak it into existence

I was at the University of Georgia's annual football coaching clinic a few years ago, and the featured speaker was Bill Belichick. Coach Belichick has been to nine super bowls as a Head Coach. Obviously, the place was packed, and I was excited to hear what he had to say. He spoke for about 30 minutes and then took some questions. I do not remember much about what he talked about, but his response to one of the questions still resonates with me. A young coach asked how he could get started in a career in professional football coaching. Coach Belichick said, "the first thing you have to do is let people know you are interested in being an NFL coach. Have you been telling people this is a goal of yours?" This answer was so simple and great. Many times, we have a vision for what we want but we do not tell people and attempt to speak it into existence. Coach Belichick went on to encourage the coach to talk to the Falcons, or any other professional organization and take whatever job he could get. In the meantime, Coach Belichick encouraged the coach to tell anyone that will listen that he wants to be an NFL coach. I thought that was great career advice, and it is so simple.

Saying something does not mean it is going to happen but speaking something into existence is a real thing. When presenting your program, you must present it as you see it becoming. Do not be scared to go out on a limb and talk about where your program is headed. Since I have taken over two struggling football programs, I found it important to always have big goals but also make them realistic. In my first meeting with the football team at Chapel Hill High in early 2008, I gave each player a copy of the 2007 Georgia High School Association state playoff bracket. I told them this was something that had never had the name "Chapel Hill" on it before and it was our goal to get our name on this page next year. At that point, I had seen none of these players perform and I had no idea if that was even a reasonable goal. However, I wanted those players to start seeing themselves as state playoff worthy. Throughout the season, I saw players with those brackets hanging in their locker. I would occasionally hear them talking about it and using the word "bracket". We made a big thing about it. That year, we became the first team to make the state playoffs in school history, and even won the first playoff game. To this day, I believe that the journey began by speaking it into existence.

Conversely, it will not always work out when you attempt to speak something into existence. Do not let that discourage you, just continue fighting and keep your vision as your compass. When I took my second Head Football Coaching job at Pickens, I tried a similar trick to that "bracket" thing with playoff wins. Pickens High had been playing football for nearly 60 years at that time and had never won a state playoff game. I came into the first meeting telling the players we were planning on getting that first playoff win that year. Turned out we did not reach that goal that year. It took us a few years, but we did eventually get a playoff win. Speaking it into existence did not work that first year, but we kept our vision for success as the compass, and eventually we were able to achieve that goal.

Talk about what you want to improve upon. If you want your team culture to be great, start talking about team culture a lot. If you want to raise more money, start talking about being one of the best fundraising teams around. Use technology to help you present your program in the light you want it to be presented. It is not enough to say these things once, they must be stated over and over and over.

Speak it into existence: How do you do it?

- ✓ **Put yourself out there** – let people know what your vision is for the team. Do not be afraid to state your goal

- ✓ **Accept it may take longer than planned** – the timetable is not always what you expected but you only fail when you give up.

- ✓ **Consistency** – it is not a one-time thing to state how you want to be perceived. It must be done repeatedly.

Conclusion

Presentation and delivery are such key ingredients in success. You must get organized in your thoughts, find the proper methods, exude confidence, and speak about your vision. These are all things that are difficult to do for most people. Keep in mind, if it were easy, everyone would succeed. It is not an easy journey to be a good presenter. You must gain experience and sometimes that only comes the hard way. After any presentation: have confidence you did the best you could, make notes on how to do it better next time, and move on.

Chris Wallace is a good friend of mine who also is currently the principal at Pickens High School. He always says, "everything comes down to relationships, communication, and presentation." We talk about leadership all of the time, and he and I both agree that these three things are the foundations for successful leadership. If you can understand the significance of these three things, you can move on to the more specific lessons. Next up: Do not get your feelings hurt so much!

Lesson Five:

Put your vision over your feelings

One of my favorite sayings is "So What, Now What?". I completely stole this saying from Dr. Kevin Elko, who worked with my alma mater, the University of Alabama, and many other professional and college teams over the years. I heard Dr. Elko speak in person at the summer conference for the Georgia Association of Educational Leaders (GAEL) and I was blown away at his perspective and attitude. I have told myself "So What, Now What?" many times since. When something bad happens, you just tell yourself "So What" and ask yourself "Now What?" and let's roll!

It is human nature to let your feelings dictate your behavior. It takes discipline to let the vision stay at the forefront of your decision making and not let feelings dictate your choices. This is true in most aspects of life, but it is especially true in leadership. When something happens that starts to hurt your feelings, try not to let it hurt your feelings. See it as an opportunity to grow, learn from it, and move on. This takes the same mental toughness and discipline that we ask from players.

Here are the important factors:
- ✓ Remember why they hired you
- ✓ Talk to yourself
- ✓ Get over trying to please everyone

Remember why they hired you

Many issues that arise for head coaches can be traced back to when they got the job. Always ask yourself: Am I doing everything I said I would do in my interview? If the answer is ever "no", you need to fix it now. Too many people try to trick people into hiring them. The truth is you should want them to want to hire you. You want your leaders to embrace you and your ideas. Keep in mind that your goal should not just be to get the job. It should be to succeed in the job. I always compare it to College Recruiting. You have athletes who want to play college football and you have athletes who just want a "signing". Some see the signing as the end of the journey. Some see the signing as the beginning of the real work. Coaches can be the same way. Are you trying to get a head coaching job as the end of some journey, or are you understanding that attaining this goal will be the beginning of the work? If you are understanding of the work, you will have a chance to make it for the long haul.

In a job interview, you are presenting a theory of how you would do the job. Turning that theory into practice can be challenging. Each job you take has a unique set of circumstances, and it is your job to mix those circumstances with your vision. Create a blended plan to achieve success. Investigate what the climate is like at a new place when they hire you and adjust. Waiting to adjust that vision later will be difficult. When I became the Head Coach at Pickens High School, they had been down for a few years. They had some success years before, and I took over for a longtime head coach at the school. It was very important that we were able to get the people who supported changing coaches, and the people who did not, to all buy in to our plan and help the program get back on the right track. I felt like the first year I was in this new position, people constantly wanted to talk about the old staff to see what I would say. I remember making it a point to be positive but try to turn the attention to the coming season. I think this was one of the best things I ever did that year. Eventually that talk waned, and we just started focusing on the task at hand. We did that without making unnecessary enemies or burning bridges before we even got started. I still work in this district today and the former coach is a man I respect and see occasionally.   When we finished the regular season 10-0 and won the school's first region championship in 2018, he was one of the first people to see me after the game and congratulate me. That meant a lot. Those decisions I made ten years ago to focus on the present and not tear down the past are still paying dividends today.

When you get hired, you have a vision and you must let that vision guide you. That does not mean it must stay the same, but the vision must be the compass. Many times, coaches allow outside factors to change their course and they slowly get away from the program they aspired to build. This process begins when feelings overtake the vision.

Remember why they hired you: How do you do it?

- ✓ **Keep the goals in mind** – coaching, or any other leadership role can be a difficult profession, but it is worth it if you can achieve your goal. Keep the end goals at the front of your mind.

- ✓ **Take the temperature of the place** – know what you are getting into when they hire you and adapt to what you immediately find out.

- ✓ **The Vision is the compass** – let your vision direct you to work to be the coach that they picked to lead the program.

Talk to yourself

In my experiences, I have found that most people listen to themselves. They feel a certain way, and they react to that feeling. To be successful as a leader you must have discipline. Talk to yourself and do not listen to yourself. This is one of many things that is easier said than done. When you have a tough loss or are dealing with some difficult off-field issues, you will feel like you are struggling, and your vision is being lost. These are the times you must talk to yourself about your purpose and goals for the program.

There will always be that voice in your head saying that you are not capable of something or that you are not good enough. The great leaders can mute that voice by purposefully talking to themselves and telling themselves what they are going to do instead of listening to that voice. This is part of being confident. Change the narrative of your self-talk. Do not let the negative voice be the loudest and be purposeful. Say to yourself what you want to be true. Listen to others but talk to yourself!

This can be an important concept when determining how to respond to issues in the program. Once something is said, it can not be taken back. It is great advice to think before you speak. Talk to yourself and ask yourself quickly, "is this something that is going to help our program grow?" If the answer is no, move on and do not say the negative comment that was entering your brain from that voice in your head. That voice can get you in trouble!

Many coaches struggle with this when it comes to being rejected for a job they wanted. They will take this rejection in an extremely negative way. There is nothing wrong with being disappointed. You put a lot of effort into the job interview and no one wants to be told they did not get a job. Take a short while to feel sorry for yourself, but do not let it last long. If this were a High School Head Football Coach job in Georgia, you could remind yourself that there were likely over one hundred applicants and they interview usually around five. You were in the 95th percentile or better if you interviewed. Remind yourself you did your best with the areas you can control. Most importantly, remind yourself that you plan on proving these people wrong. Make them wish they had hired you. Get back to work and when you do get a job like that, be ready and make this school wish they had hired you! It is a privilege to be considered and it is a journey to get to the destination you desire. Go into the next interview with this attitude: they will either select you for the position or they will not, and you do not have the say. What you do control is how you navigate the process and how you present yourself. Spend all your time on this and do the best you can. If you did the best you can and they offer you the job, prove them right! If they do not accept you for the job, you did the best you could and you did not want to be anywhere that did not want you!

This advice works for any kind of rejection or doubt. Do not let them get you down. Talk to yourself and prove them wrong.

Talk to yourself: How do you do it?

✓ **Daily Decision** – do not dwell on yesterday's success or failure. Discipline is a daily decision.

✓ **Listen to others, talk to yourself** – try not to listen to that voice inside you telling you that you cannot do it; talk to yourself and say you can.

✓ **Think before you speak** – let your comments roll through your head before you speak; especially to parents, players, admin and in formal meetings.

✓ **Prove them wrong if they do not want you; prove them right if they do** – focus on the things you can control and talk to yourself about doing the best you can.

Get over trying to please everyone

If I have learned anything in a lifetime of coaching and athletic administration, it is that if you try to please everyone, you will please no one. Instead of worrying about "pleasing" anyone, just stay focused on your vision and purpose.

Sometimes it will be aligned with other people's and sometimes it will not.

When someone is criticizing you, it is very natural to get defensive. Try not to do this. Instead, try to listen to criticism and ask yourself if there is some merit to the claim. If there is, take responsibility and talk about ways to do better next time. Is the criticism a misunderstanding? If so, clear things up. If the criticism is completely made up, calmly state your rebuttal. See criticism as a chance to get better. It may force you to defend yourself, but you need to have defenses for everything you do.

Consistency is the hallmark of excellence. Doing the same thing repeatedly is how you build a reputation and build your program. It is especially important to be consistent when being a leader. Even if it does not align with your friends on certain issues, you must stick to your principles and handle things the same for everyone, as much as possible. Everyone that has ever coached has been accused of "playing favorites". It should not bother you that people say that; it should bother you if it is true. Are you giving out different punishments to people on the team for the same issue? Are you treating some assistant coaches different than others? It is easy to accidently do these things. You must try to be consistent in everything you do as a leader.

You are never going to make everyone happy. Ironically, I was reminded about this principle in the first regular season game I was the Head Football Coach, and again in the last. Our first game at Chapel Hill was against Lithia Springs. It was on the road and Lithia Springs was a big favorite. Chapel Hill had really struggled. We come out and jump on them early with a double pass and a fake punt and win the game. It was euphoric. People were so happy. Chapel Hill was 1-0. It was a short bus ride back, but I was feeling rather good about myself. The players were having a great time on the bus and I was happy for them as they had not won much in their careers. Calling the fake punt and the double pass at the right time turned out to be great moves. I was young and naïve so I assumed no one would have a problem with me! When we got back to the school as I approached my office door, I saw a lady waiting for me. She asked to speak to me. It was someone's mother that did not get to play much in the game. She was not happy and let me have it. Now, that does not seem like much, but at the time I was really shocked that she was so upset considering we had just won this huge game and her son was a part of it. Fast forward many years later and we are in the last regular season game I ever coached at Pickens. We win the game and finish the first 10-0 season in school history. Again, the game was on the road and as I am going back to leave, I get approached by a player's father, also upset about playing time.

The reality is, there was nothing we could have done as a staff to make everyone happy. If those individuals had played more, it just would have made different people upset. The key is to focus on your vision and stay consistent so you can handle these situations the best you can.

Get over pleasing everyone: How do you do it?

✓ **Take criticism as a chance to get better** – instead of taking it personal, see any criticism as a chance to either improve, clear up a misunderstanding, or defend your actions. These are all traits you need to be able to do.

✓ **Consistency** – stay consistent in your principles; especially in dealing with player discipline, players playing other sports, admin, etc.

✓ **Realize you do not control other people's actions** – ultimately, you have no control over people getting their feelings hurt. You control whether you let them hurt your feelings.

Conclusion

Putting your vision over your feelings is easy to say but difficult to do. This is a thing that takes time and discipline to master. I personally work at this daily and still have plenty of room to grow. As an Athletic Director and Head Football Coach I have dealt with hundreds of things that fit this chapter and yet I am still working on it daily. Keep talking to yourself about your vision and the methods you are going to use to improve. Use criticism as a chance to get better and ultimately realize that you cannot please everyone.

If you can work on not getting your feelings hurt, it will be much easier to succeed at the next lesson: Avoiding petty problems.

Lesson Six:

Avoid petty problems

It is usually not the big things that make for leadership failure. There are many more tiny "landmines" out there that you must avoid in order to become a successful leader. It is difficult to stay the course and not let little, petty things get in the way of plans, relationships, communication, presentation, and feelings. This lesson focuses on two ways to avoid petty problems:

1. **Be preemptive:** This means you must avoid petty problems by addressing them before they become problems. You must be able to "see the future".

2. **Pick your battles:** You will not win every battle. Do not argue with every parent, administrator, other sports' coach, etc. Decide which are big problems and which are petty problems. A key question to ask

yourself is: Will this affect us winning a game or growing our program to help students? If the answer is no, why are you spending time worrying or debating it? If the answer is yes, then I guess you must cultivate a strategy to help you get back on course.

Here are the important factors:
- ✓ See the future
- ✓ Make rules you will enforce
- ✓ Follow up
- ✓ Quit trying to be right

See the future

I told players all the time that I could "see the future". Obviously, I do not have magical powers, but I could predict the future most of the time based on experience. I recognized that if I said "this", they were likely going to say "that"; and if this player did "this" then it was going to lead to "that". No one is right all the time on this and there are exceptions to every rule, but it is important to success to recognize what could be coming. Being observant to non-verbal cues and body language can also help you to "see the future".

Here are some examples of things you need to recognize:

- ✓ A player is frustrated about playing time
- ✓ A good young player is coming up to the varsity but may not get immediate success
- ✓ A player is going to have to play too early and will struggle but we need them to continue developing
- ✓ A player is jealous of the success of another player
- ✓ An assistant coach is not happy with his or her current responsibilities on the team.
- ✓ A parent has been helping a lot, but their child may not get to play much
- ✓ A parent is determined their child will play a position they will likely not end up playing
- ✓ Administrator is not happy with you
- ✓ The coach of another sport is becoming frustrated with dealing with your sport
- ✓ A local business partner does not think you appreciate their financial support

If you can recognize these things before major issues arise, you can address them and have an even stronger relationship with those involved and an even stronger program. Pay attention to all the little things in the program. The entire program is like a garden, it must be cultivated daily. You can not just show up and work a few times a year. You must do many things every day to cultivate growth and see real change.

One way I tried to "see the future" was in our individual player meetings. For example, I would take a player that had a great freshman season on the freshman team and when we sat down before his sophomore season, I may tell him a story about how sophomore year can be tough. I would likely tell him that most good players struggle in their sophomore year. He may be good enough to play on the varsity but may be a backup and get a lot of reps in practice but not many in the game. He would also have to be on the scout team. I would then tell that same player that although sophomore year is tough, if he can work to get better through this year, his junior and senior years will be amazing. He will be one of the best players in the region! When you tell this story to a player in April, they look at you a little perplexed. Why is this man saying all of this to me? Who is he to question my ability to play? I understand their perplexity and since it is only April and football is played in the Fall, they do not let it bother them much. We then move on to talk about more specific things like their strength and speed numbers, and how to get them up.

Fast forward to the season and that same player is on the scout team and having a hard time. I would just walk up to him, put my arm around him, smile, and say, "remember when I told you sophomore year was kind of hard?" He would say "yes sir Coach, you were right." I would then say, "but remember what else I told you. I told you that you were a great player and if you could make it through this that you would be one of the best players in our region. I still believe that and believe it now more than ever. Just keep working and don't get discouraged." He would again say "yes sir", but he would remember that conversation. If I was right about it being tough, then I may be right about him being one of the best players in the region. This same player now understands his role on the team, and he is prepared to step in when needed and to be a leader for us in the future.

Now, let us paint the picture for that same young man if you never have a conversation with him about the future. You would be bragging about him in the coaching office as a great freshman player, know he would likely be a backup this year, and see him as a future leader in your program, but you never sat down and told him the year was going to be hard. You assume he knows he is a good player and he knows you care about him. After several months on the scout team and not getting to play, he starts complaining at home that the "coach doesn't like him". You have no idea this is going on because he is still respectful to your face. Then after a few more weeks of him not playing on Friday night, struggling on the scout team, and not corresponding with the head coach, he is not at practice one day. It turns out he has quit. You find him and try to talk him back on the team. You let him know that he is going to be a future leader. He is not as sure if he can believe you or not, but he does reluctantly return. He may have a great career from then on, but he may also be a guy that struggles in the next off-season and never really reaches his maximum potential.

I do not want this story to appear as though it is the coach's fault that did not have the exact discussion I had with players. I also do not want you to think that if you have that discussion it means that every player will reach his maximum potential. All of this simply means you are attempting to "see the future" and when you are right, it can have some incredibly positive repercussions for your program. If you can see problems before they arise, you can avoid the petty things that deteriorate your program. Here are some other examples of being pre-emptive and seeing the future:

➢ *A player is frustrated about playing time* – If you can catch them and talk to them before they approach you about it, it will be more effective. Let them know where they stand and let them know how they can improve. Also, always let them know that you care about them as a person way more than a player and their playing time has nothing to do with that.

➢ *A player is going to have to play too early and we need him to keep developing* – You need to talk to that player before the season and check in with him during the season. Let him know that you are proud of him and the work he is doing now will make him great in the future. Find some old stories of NFL guys that struggled early to motivate him.

> ➤ *A player is jealous of the success of another player* – This is hard to correct but if you think it may happen, go ahead and address it. It may seem futile to bring up something that may not even be there, but I would just have an informal talk (at practice, in the cafeteria, etc.) with the player and let him know he is doing a great job and do not worry about any accolades others are getting. Just worry about what you can control and keep working hard.

> ➤ *An assistant coach is not happy with his/her current responsibilities on the team* – Use your annual formal meetings to help with this but if you sense one of them is not happy, call them in. Talk to them about where they stand and how they can improve. I would use these chances to be honest and not to promise things you may not be able to deliver in the future as that will make the situation eventually worse and not better.

> ➤ *A parent has been helping the team a lot, but their child will not get to play much* – Try to slip in as many times as possible how much you like their child and want the best for him when there is no issue. Make sure you have not promised anything to the parent or player and when eventually they want to talk about the subject, remind them that you care about their child. You just must play the best players and you understand they are frustrated.

> ➤ *A parent is determined their child should play a position they will likely not play* – if they are not making these comments to you, I would not pay much attention to them. If they are making them to you, you should address it. Sit them down and let them know

that with all players, you will give them a chance to play where they want. If they are great, you will be ecstatic; if they do not play well in that position, you will have to move them somewhere else that better fits the team. Waiting to have this conversation after they are already frustrated can be the most difficult way.

➢ *Administrator is not happy with you* – If you coach long enough, you will have to deal with some administration issues. I got extremely fortunate that I did not have many, but I do know it happens all the time and it is not always anyone's fault. You can be pre-emptive in many ways here: Always keep the admin informed and let them know what is going on if you have issues they may have to deal with as well. The more you can communicate with them before it becomes an issue the more this will not be an issue. If you hear they are not happy with you, contact them. I would always confront this issue. Set up a meeting and go talk to them. Do not text or email, have a face-to-face meeting and ask what you are struggling with and what you can do better. Put the ball in their court to let you know how to improve. It will be much easier to handle this if you "see the future".

➢ *The coach of another sport is becoming frustrated with your sport* – this inevitably will occur at some point as well. You will likely get this impression by non-verbal cues or someone will tell you about it. If this happens, treat it the same was as with the administrator. Contact them to set up a meeting and talk to them about the issue. Put the ball in their court and be proactive.

> ➤ *A local business partner does not feel like you appreciate their support* – Write thank you notes annually to all your local sponsors and financial partners. This may seem like no big deal, but I did this every year and it would take weeks. It is still worth it. Make sure you brag on them every chance you get. Once they develop this relationship it will be hard to correct, so try to be pre-emptive. If it gets to this point, call them in and have a face-to-face meeting with them and talk to them about how much you appreciate their support and ask what you can do in the future to show it better.

See the future: How do you do it?

✓ **Have tough discussions with players before anything happens** – always be alert to opportunities to let someone know when you think the future may be challenging. It is much easier to have this conversation when things are cordial than after they have been frustrated.

✓ **Be observant** – recognize when players, coaches, admin, parents are acting differently and try to talk to them.

✓ **Initiate the conversation** – anytime you can be the one to bring up a tough issue without them having to bring it up to you, it will be much easier to move forward.

✓ **Put the ball in their court** – always bring up the issue to them and ask what they have is their issue and ask how it can be handled better in the future.

Make rules you will enforce

A key mistake I have witnessed over the years is coaches coming into a new environment intent on "fixing" the place by making them "work harder" or "take care of the little things". Do not get me wrong, those things are extremely important, and those coaches mean well. The issue is they pick things to focus on that will likely be difficult to enforce all year.

Imagine if you take over a new team that is struggling and you have a long list of team rules. One of them is they must hang their helmet on the left side of the locker every day at the end of practice. When someone ask you "why" they are doing that, you respond "because I said so" or "because we are going to do every little thing exactly right." Those answers are not wrong. But it does create an environment where you have now based your relationships with those players on you going into the locker room after every practice and checking every locker, every day. My experience has been that coaches come up with plans like this and enforce them for a while but eventually the attention to it wanes. When this happens, kids subconsciously do not have as much regard for the rules, little things, or working harder. Ironically, the thing you were trying to fix is the thing that is now worse.

So instead of coming up with a long list of rules, focus on one or two things. Make it something that affects winning and build from there. If the players do a great job with those few things, then add some more later. I tried to focus on these rules...

Off the field
- ❖ Be where you are supposed to be
- ❖ Do Right

On the field
- ❖ Give great effort
- ❖ Have a great attitude

Those seem generic for a reason. We could easily enforce those rules. We focused on those four things. If it did not fall under those rules, I did not worry too much about it. That does not mean that other stuff is not important, but we needed to have clear expectations. I would rather have a few rules we could enforce, than a bunch of rules we could not enforce.

You earn so much respect from players when you take a common-sense approach. This goes for off-field rules and on-field rules. The common on-field mistake is getting onto a player for doing something they obviously did not do on purpose. This includes, but is not limited to, fumbling the ball, throwing an interception, and missing a tackle. Otherwise good coaches sometimes make a mistake when these things happen by yelling and demeaning the player. Absolutely, you should correct the player but do not make them feel like they did it on purpose. If they fumbled, tell them to carry the ball high and tight with 4 points of pressure. If they threw an interception, ask "what did you see?". If they missed a tackle, talk to them about their angle or their approach. Student-athletes will respect you so much more if the feedback is meaningful. They know when they have messed up and it does no good to redundantly point it out. With that being said, I sometimes lost my mind about things that involved attitude and effort. Players knew the phrase "is that the best you can do?" If the answer was "no" it was not a great atmosphere at practice for a short period of time. The players knew there was no excuse for a bad attitude or poor effort.

Make rules you can enforce: How do you do it?

- ✓ **Common sense approach** – players, coaches, and parents will all appreciate a common-sense approach to team rules.

- ✓ **Consistency in procedures** – you must follow through with all rules you come up with; if you like a lot of rules, you must enforce all of them.

- ✓ **Rules that are simple and everyone understands** – have on-field and off-field rules that the players know by heart.

Follow up

A key to building the trust and respect that turns programs around is following up on any negative reinforcement. If there was a time when effort or attitude was lacking and I had to get on a young man, I always made a point to find the player later in that day and pump them up. This is a great chance to remind them of the team rules. I would say something like, "you know I love you and want to see you be as successful as you can be. You know we only get on to you about your attitude and your effort. We do not get on to you for messing up. Just give us your best, that is all we want." Most athletes respond well to that and move on. This is a huge part of making your program a success. You must have high standards and get on to people for bad attitude and effort, but you cannot afford to lose respect or excitement while doing so.

You can follow up on adult issues as well. If you have any issues with parents, coaches, or administrators, follow up with them. Let them know about your passion for the program and your desire to work with them in the future. These are some of the times when you can really grow your program. Show some humility and let them know it is not personal.

Follow Up: How do you do it?

- ✓ **Make a note** – whether mental or physical, make a note when you have an issue with a player and make sure you follow up with them and let them know why you have the best intentions.

✓ **Make sure they know it is not personal** – take some time to explain yourself when you follow up and stay humble. Show them that it is not personal and any procedures you are following is for the betterment of the program.

Quit trying to be right

People try so hard to be right. One of my go-to lines to coaches is, "do you want to win or do you want to be right?" So often in leadership you come across people who mostly care about showing you they are right even at the expense of winning. In this case "winning" does not necessarily only mean winning the games, but also advancing the program. An example of this would be if you are able to correct a parent/player/coach, but in doing so it is going to slow down the advancement of the program. What good does it do to be "right"? Let the other person feel like they got the best of you occasionally, especially on the things that do not matter for advancement of the program. Then when you have a real issue, you can argue about it and it will not be perceived as something you do constantly. Being a leader is a tough enough job already without adding new landmines yourself because you dig a deeper and deeper hole trying to be "right".

I dealt with this as an Athletic Director even more than I did as Head Football Coach. Coaches would come in and be upset at someone because of something that was said, and I would usually ask "why does that matter?" They would reply something that started with, "I just don't like them thinking

_____." I would have to remind them that thoughts do not win games. Who cares what others think if your vision is still intact? Only argue when it is making the program go backwards.

Now, do not get me wrong, I also like to be right! I would be a hypocrite if I did not include this disclaimer. My brother Michael and I will argue about anything, but when it came to the football program, I could let other people win if it meant we were advancing the program. Remember, keep your vision ahead of your feelings!

There is one easy way to limit the number of times you must admit when you are wrong: do not make stuff up! It is alright if you do not know the answer to something. In my career I have encountered people who refused to admit they were wrong or made a mistake. This is a huge flaw. If you are like this, work on this now. If you misspoke, do not dig a deeper hole trying to defend yourself. Simply say, I was wrong, I misunderstood, or whatever other phrase would be appropriate.

There is no shame in saying the phrase, "I do not know" as long as you follow it up with, "but I will find out". If you get asked a question you do not know the answer to, simply say you do not know. You would really think this would not be necessary advice, but I see it all the time and I have experienced the consequences. Trying to make up some half-educated excuse of an answer is only going to fracture your relationship with people when they realize you did not know what you were talking about. There is power in saying you do not know. It makes you appear human. Do not forget to add in the "but I will find out" phrase. No one wants to spend time talking to someone that knows nothing but if you say you do not know and will find out, people will respect you. Then make yourself a note to find answers and follow up. This is a much better response than making something up that sounds fine in the meeting but is not correct. People will appreciate your willingness to admit you did not know and they will appreciate you cared enough to follow up. Of course, they would also appreciate an accurate answer!

Many times, being right and winning are on the same page: what is true of one will be true of the other. Those few times when they are on opposite ends, fight the human nature to have to be right. Ask yourself if arguing this is going to help your program. If it is, then keep arguing. If it is not, let them win. They can have this battle. You are looking to win the war.

<u>Quit trying to be right: How do you do it?</u>

✓ **Admit when you are wrong** – there is no shame in admitting when you made a mistake. It takes a real leader to humble themselves and admit when they were wrong.

✓ **It is alright to not know** – when you do not know the answer to something, say you do not know. Do not make up answers to appear to understand. This is a good example of putting off work. It will be easier in the short-term but lead to issues in the long-term

✓ **Do you want to be right or do you want to win?** Pick a side. You cannot always have both.

Conclusion

Being able to avoid the petty problems that will be thrown in front of you constantly will be a big help in your program reaching its maximum potential. Avoid the "landmines" out there and be successful!

If you can center your thinking to focus on your vision and avoid petty problems, you can start to focus on your program. The next lesson was one of the most impactful for me personally: Focus on what you have and not what you do not have.

Lesson Seven:

Focus on what you have

When you are struggling, it is extremely easy to focus on what you do not have instead of what you do have. Worrying about things you can not control is a common error. Because I was fortunate enough to be the Head Football Coach at two places that were struggling and have success, I am often asked what I feel like the most important things are to making this happen. I always answer this lesson: Focus on what you have and not what you wish you had. I learned this in my first year as a Head Coach. When I went to Chapel Hill High School after the 2007 season there was a lot of work to do.

Here was the landscape that I remember as I took the job:

* ❖ The football team had not had any on-field success and the confidence was extremely low.

- ❖ We did not have great facilities. There was one boys' locker room that we shared with basketball and soccer.
- ❖ We got parts of 3 different middle schools but none exclusively making it incredibly difficult to build the program.
- ❖ It was difficult to raise money in the recession and the procedures by which they ran the athletic department booster club made it difficult for football.
- ❖ The other sports had performed well. The Track and Cross Country programs had won multiple state championships. Basketball and baseball had years of successful teams.

When I started out it was easy to complain about the facilities and money. It was easy to catch myself being jealous of the success of the other sports. It was easy to worry that we would not be able to win with these players who had not won before. All of these were natural thoughts. As a new Head Coach, I was struggling with how to deal with all of these things. Dr. Jason Branch was the principal that hired me. He was a great leader and has since gone on to be a superintendent in a large district in Georgia. I went into Dr. Branch's office and began to tell him all the things that were worrying me. I will never forget his response. He said, "Coach, do you have a question?" This conversation is something I am sure he does not remember but I do. I was in the principal's office complaining. I was simply bringing problems with no solutions. The man who took a chance on a young football coach did not need to hear me airing my grievances and wasting his time.

As a PE teacher I spent a lot of time in the gym. After a few days in the gym it was evident we had some good athletes. It was evident there were some good coaches there. I got to know those other coaches and they were very encouraging. It was easy to see why their teams won. If all these programs had won at this school, why not football? I was gaining confidence that we could really make this happen!

A few weeks later, another key moment occurred. I was talking to the coaches of the other sports. I asked them why they thought the football team had struggled while the other sports had performed well. I remember the answer they all had: "Everyone that has come in here has focused on what they did not have and not on what they did have." This is when I began using this phrase. It resonated with me.

I started to spend my time focusing on ways to get the best athletes to play football. I started to focus on ways to get the best athletes on the field out in space so we could use their athleticism to our advantage. I took every chance I could to pick the brains of all the other successful coaches at the school on what they were doing to help their teams. None of this changed the fact that we still had to share a locker room with basketball and soccer, and we did not have a great structure with the middle schools. But I rarely thought about those things. This was in the early days of the spread offense in Georgia and we were running some version of this. They had not run this before. That could have been a negative, but we just focused on the fact that they had no bad habits. They were happy to be out there because we were happy to be out there. It would have been so easy to focus on our inadequacies and not on the good.

Here are the important factors:
- ✓ Make it nice
- ✓ Be Self-aware
- ✓ Worry about what you can control

Make it nice

One of the first ways to "focus on what you have" is to make whatever you have as nice as it can be. It was always irritating as an Athletic Director to have a coach complaining about his or her facility being inadequate, and they did not do a great job keeping the place they did have clean. Why would we spend money on bigger or nicer facilities when you have struggled to maintain what you have? If you have an average car, keep it clean and make it look like an above-average car. Whatever you have, make it nice!

When I first moved to Pickens County, one of the first things we did was put up pictures on the walls of the field house. Some people may have thought I was losing my mind. The team was struggling off the field and we had no money. Why was I worried about decorating? I wanted to put pics and posters up for two reasons: to show the history of the place and to make the place look better. It did not cost much, and we even had some local businesses help us. I also printed off some things on regular paper and laminated them. We did anything that was inexpensive, but made the place look better.

We did not complain that we had no money. Instead we made the place look as nice as it could be and then asked for money! My first year at Pickens we had 35 sponsors. We were happy with that number as it was a slight improvement from what they had the year before. By my last year, we had over 150! This was such a source of pride for me. Not just because we had the money that we needed to run the program, but because people chose to give us their money. I did not take that lightly. The community believed that we would take their money and use it to help kids and make our program great. I really believe this type of support started to grow when we began making the most of what we had.

Years before, in my first year at Chapel Hill, we found the cheapest Nike uniforms we could buy and found a way to pay for them because the players wanted to wear Nike. They were not as expensive as the players thought and we had to buy new uniforms anyway, but we took whatever we had and tried to make it appear as nice as possible. We had a very small budget at Chapel Hill but I do not remember our players feeling like they were slighted because we made the most of what we had and kept everything as nice as we could keep it. The same principle held true: take whatever you have and make it as nice as it can be.

Make it nice: How do you do it?

✓ **Keep it clean** – whatever you do have, make it as clean and well-kept as it can be. No one wants to give you something nice if you cannot take care of what you have.

✓ **Do the cheap, easy repairs** – keep your eyes open to small things you can do that make your place and program look nicer.

✓ **Aesthetics are important** – even minor things that make it look more official like logos, colors, etc. are important. Find ways within your budget to make your facilities as nice as they can be.

Be self-aware

You have to be able to know where you stand. This can be interpreted in so many different ways. Being self-aware can mean any of the following:

- ✓ Realizing how you sound
- ✓ Realizing how you are perceived
- ✓ Realizing where you stand with people

One of the main ways you can be self-aware is to implement a no complaining rule. There are no excuses and no complaints. All excuses and complaints will do is make it appear that you do not understand where you are and where you are headed. Excuse making is a natural thing. We have defense mechanisms that make this a challenge. Fight that urge to complain and make excuses. You will be glad you did! Whatever it is you wanted to complain about, I can assure you, some people have it worse than you. When you start complaining, the person you are talking to will immediately hear you and think that you are being any of the following: spoiled, selfish, disrespectful, etc.

Work with the other sports in the building. Be aware of how it looks when you act like your group is better or more important. Try to see things from the point of view of others and only pick battles that are worth fighting. If it is not a battle worth fighting, cater to the other group. Give them what they want so you will hopefully, eventually get what you want. Realize when you are arguing with another group you may be perceived as selfish. They are immediately going to think of all the times you "got" something and feel like you are in the way of them getting something. An example of this was when we had our early season practices during pre-planning. This is the time when teachers must work but students are not in the building. Since we had workouts in the morning all summer, our coaches would have preferred to have practice in the morning and miss some of their teaching obligations. I could have asked the principal to give us the time and let us practice, but even if the principal agreed, it was a bad look. I wanted our guys to be like all the other teachers. We moved those practices to start after teaching was over for the day. I have seen other teams do this differently and there is nothing wrong with that if they have approval, but it was not one of the battles I wanted to fight. I tried to be aware of how that would be perceived by others.

Another way you need to be self-aware is in showing loyalty to those that have helped you. Be loyal to your fellow coaches, administrators, and community. As mentioned earlier, one of my great friends along the way as a coach is Sam Wigington. Sam was the other person that was considered for the Head Coaching job when I got the job at Pickens. He had gone to school there and had been the longest tenured assistant coach on the staff when I arrived. These individuals are often the first to go when the regime changes. One of the first questions I asked Sam when we first sat down to talk was about the old coach. I wanted to hear what he had to say. He was very complimentary. I saw this as a positive. I knew the team had struggled and there had been some issues, but Sam refused to talk bad about that coach. He just kept talking about the future and us working together. This is being self-aware. If you go in and bash a coach, administrator, or parent to someone you barely know, they should immediately realize you will do the same thing to them. What I found in Sam that day was loyalty. He was loyal to the old coach and he was loyal to me. I knew I could count on him!

Be self-aware: How do you do it?

- ✓ **No complaining** – it brings no value to complain and you usually come across spoiled or selfish. Be grateful for what you have and make it better.

- ✓ **Do not act like you are above anything** – take initiative to help other groups in the school and other organizations. Never act like your group is immune to doing something.

- ✓ **Be loyal** – keep in mind that most leaders understand if you talk bad about someone behind their back, you will likely do it to them. This is a major way to lose respect.

Worry about what you can control

You control your attitude and your effort. Honestly, you control little else. Being able to compartmentalize worry is a key ingredient in achieving success. For example, if you forgot to prepare for the booster club meeting tonight and your best player got suspended from school, you should spent more time worrying about that booster club meeting because you have much more control over that than you do a player's school discipline. In this example, most people sit around and fret about the player issue, and the booster club meeting becomes an even bigger mess. Ask yourself, can I control this? If the answer is yes, fix it. If the answer is no, do the best you can and try to focus on something else.

When bad things happen, and they will, see your challenges as opportunities. We really preached the attitude and effort theme over and over to our teams. I really think this was one of the many reasons why we had success at two places that had been struggling. We were able to win games where we were down 14 points early or able to score after giving up a big play because we were more focused on things that mattered in the moment. One of our better coaching jobs came in 2010 when we started the year 0-4 and came back to play for the sub-region championship. We had such success in 2008 and 2009 that it was difficult to make a schedule. We had a very difficult early season schedule with a young team. We struggled but we never lost focus of our attitude and effort. We quickly won the next four in a row to get right back in the region championship discussion. That team ended with the worst record of any team I ever coached but I was so proud of them. They never gave up! We lost that sub-region championship game but the next year we played the same team for the same sub-region championship and we won! Many of the lessons from that 0-4 start in 2010 helped us win our sub-region in 2011.

Worrying about what you can control, having a great attitude in the tough times, and giving your best effort is the recipe for success. Our phrase was "make them quit". That was what we focused on instead of just telling them "play with heart." Maybe it was just semantics but I liked this phrase better. We wanted to give great effort and focus on the next play the entire game. We wanted to make that guy across from us quit. We did not worry about the first play or the tenth play. We wanted to see when he would quit and then go harder and harder. This phrase seemed to resonate with the players. "Make 'em quit" was a staple of the halftime talks. The reason I used this mantra so much was it always applied, regardless if we were ahead, behind, or tied. It was all about the next play and all about attitude and effort. This is something you can control!

You should spend little time trying to change on things you do not control. You should, however, spend plenty of time working on how you react to those things. What you do control is how you navigate the process and move on from any event that has altered your plan. Spend your time doing the best you can do. All anyone can ask for is your best.

Worry about what you control: How do you do it?

✓ **See your challenges as opportunities** – anytime you have something bad happen, re-focus yourself on what you can control and see this as an opportunity to grow. Your mindset will determine everything.

✓ **Realize you determine your attitude** – it is a great moment when you finally realize that you, and only you, determine your attitude and how hard you will work.

✓ **Find a mantra for attitude and effort** – if you like talking about "heart", "making them quit" or something else, find a mantra that you can say over and over when you need to remind yourself to give great effort and have a positive attitude.

Conclusion

You must take whatever you have and make the best of it. Stay positive and keep your focus on what you do have. The key to focusing on what you have is to make whatever you have as nice as it can be. Be self-aware of how you sound, and only worry about the things you can control. It sounds simple, but this can be exceedingly difficult. As humans, we have some natural tendencies that work against these ideas. We must be prepared to fight the urges that will lure you away from your goals.

If you have a good understanding of all the things in these first seven lessons, you may think you are close to having it figured out. Many times, I thought I had finally made a breakthrough only to realize the next lesson: You never have it all figured out!

Lesson Eight:

You never have it all figured out

Just when you think you have everything figured out, there is always someone there to remind you that you do not. This is true no matter what level of success you have had in the past. This is true in all aspects of your program. Never let yourself believe you have the perfect way of doing something. Instead embrace other ideas, evaluate your ideas truthfully, and continue to grow throughout your career. The coaches that grasp this philosophy stay the most current and successful as they do not get caught in the "way we have always done it" mode!

This happened to me as an offensive play caller all the time. We would have a great formation or play that would work for a while and we would think we discovered something and then the next week the opposing defense would have something to stop it. This is a metaphor for everything we did in the program. If you ever think you have it all figured out, it means you have quit growing and you need to do something else.

Most of the guys that coached offense with me probably got tired of me slightly tweaking the formations or terminology. I was always looking for that perfect plan. It used to irritate me that I would think of something new and want to change all of it again. I kept thinking to myself, "If we make these changes then we finally will not have to change again." Eventually I realized that the constant tweaking and evaluating was part of the reason we were successful. It was not the perfect plan we needed, but rather it was the journey to get to the perfect plan that was needed. We would never reach the destination but attempting to get there was one of the reasons we had success.

Here are the important factors:
- ✓ Think like a rookie
- ✓ Work to a standard
- ✓ Self-Evaluation

Think like a rookie

"Football is a tough game", "Football is a great game", "Football is more than a game".... These are all mantras I heard growing up in Foley, Alabama and continue to hear. I loved football growing up. My family loved football and when I graduated from the University of Alabama all I wanted to do was be a coach. I did not care if I ever became the Head Coach. I just wanted to Coach. I took the first job I was offered at Sequoyah High School about an hour north of Atlanta. I had never lived outside of Alabama and I did not know anyone in the entire state of Georgia. I did not care; I just needed a job. There was one hang up: they did not have any football coaching positions.

They offered me a job teaching Social Studies and told me I needed to talk to the Head Football Coach about helping with football as they did not think they had any openings. I went down to the field house and met Coach Sid Maxwell. Coach Maxwell told me I could come help with their morning workouts and they would find something for me to do but I would not get a supplement. I was fine with that as I just wanted to help. I was so happy to be a real coach!

I was happy being on the team and was willing to do whatever was needed to help the team win. I am willing to bet that most coaches felt the same way when they started out. As you progress in coaching, it is easy to forget about that "rookie" attitude. You start to slowly get away from the satisfaction of being a part of the team. If you want to be as successful as you can be, you must continue to think like a rookie. When you are a rookie you have the excitement but not the knowledge. Many times, by the time you are a veteran you have the knowledge but have lost the joy that comes with being a rookie. Imagine how great you could be if you maintain that excitement and love for coaching after you gain the knowledge and experience!

To think like a rookie, you must stay motivated to get better and gain knowledge. Always take the opportunities presented to you to talk with others about your craft. Listen to what they do and ask questions. Most new coaches do this, but you can do it as a veteran as well. Experience coaches frequently underestimate the value of learning, especially from the young coaches. Do not carry an attitude that you know it all. I have seen coaches with multiple championships sit down and study a new way of doing things that was being presented by someone that has won zero championships. That is an indicator of why those coaches are so successful! Have some initiative to listen, learn, study, and attend clinics. Do your research and take as many professional development opportunities as you can.

Think like a Rookie: How do you do it?

- ✓ **Stay inspired to improve** – keep the rookie spirit even after you have some knowledge. Always keep that excitement to learn and grow in your profession.

- ✓ **Remember how it felt to be a rookie** – no matter how long ago it has been, always remember how you felt when you first started out. Remember why you got into the profession. Keep that rookie attitude and excitement!

- ✓ **Learn from everyone** – you can learn from coaches or leaders older or younger than you. Do not assume because someone has less experience than you that you could not learn something from them.

Work to a Standard

Little did I know that single decision to accept that teaching job at Sequoyah High School, and beg to help with football, would put me on the course to where I am today. I had never heard of Sid Maxwell or Sequoyah High School, but knew I wanted to be a coach. I could have been starting a job at a place with a good or bad staff as I had no idea. Turned out it was a fantastic staff! In my time at Sequoyah we had ten current, former, or future head coaches on staff: Sid Maxwell, Ray Face, Al Morrell, Ed Koester, Travis Mozingo, Louis Daniel, Oz Price, Cory Nix, Jeff Nelson, and me. It was great place to learn. The main thing that Coach Maxwell and the others at Sequoyah taught me was to always work to a standard.

As a young coach, I assumed we just coached to have more points than the team we were about to play. That is the perspective you often have as a player. Ray Face was a longtime Head Coach and served as the Defensive Coordinator. I coached the Defensive Backs in my first few years so I worked closely with Coach Face and Coach Maxwell. They were tough, but they treated me fair and took me under their wings. They taught me to focus on the play and strive to be great on each play at each position, regardless if the play was successful or not. I was so impressed with how we worked to our standard. I started grading practice video and sending Coach Maxwell full reports daily. I am sure he really studied them and did not throw them away! Regardless, it gave me an understanding of why we needed to do it perfect if we wanted to achieve our goal of being the best we could be. Our goal was not to win; it was to be our best. This was a new concept to me, but I embraced it and embodied it for the next two decades!

The plan was to always show improvement. To work to get better after success and after failure. We wanted to take pride in our program and put the team ahead of ourselves. Every coach on the staff should have felt a responsibility for the success or failure of the total football program. We were working towards perfection. We would never get there but on the way, there would be some amazing things happen!

Work to a Standard: How do you do it?

✓ **Show improvement** – always be working to get better regardless of the score, situation, or positioning

✓ **Take pride in the process** – understand there will be failure and you must take pride in your program and the process to greatness

✓ **Strive for perfection** – you will never get there but you will get somewhere close if you keep striving for the standard and not the scoreboard.

Self-Evaluation

There is no better way to understand this lesson than to self-evaluate. It has already been mentioned multiple times in this book that you should make notes and evaluate your plan often. This self-evaluation can occur through making small notes, individual changes, or total program evaluation.

Making notes has been such a big part of any success I have had as a coach or AD. After an event is over, I would make notes on how it went and what we can do better next time. This is something that started out small and grew over the years. I really think this is the best way to improve because it is fresh on your mind. You learn from your mistakes and inefficiencies and will try to not repeat. Make frequent notes and refer to these notes often.

However, your notes are only useful if you put them into action. You need to have a system to take your notes and add them to your plan. I believe in written plans and procedures as I think that is the best way to manage them. I would update those plans with my notes as they happened. Then at the end of the year, you would have a new "manual" for the next year with all the different aspects of the program. For example, we did a "Meet the Dragons" night where we invited all teams K-12th grade, cheer, band to perform in the first week of padded practice. This was a fundraiser but also just a fun community event. I would have a document with 2-3 pages stating what we were doing and what our procedures would be for the event. After the event was over, I would take a few minutes and read through that document and make changes for next year. I may not look at it much again until we start preparing for next year's event and then I would read that again. It was a tedious process, but it kept us evolving in a positive way.

I also believed it was important to do a total program evaluation annually. I took all our written manuals and procedures and reviewed them. I sent a detailed survey to each coach. It is extremely easy to use Google Forms or some other survey company to make a survey and send to your people. The survey was simple but long. It was centered around the following three questions:

- ➢ What went well this year regarding _____?
- ➢ What do you need to work on regarding _____?
- ➢ Rate _____ on a scale from 1-10 (ten being the best)

Mostly, it was just these three questions repeated with the "blanks" filled in for each of the following categories:

- ➢ Total Program
- ➢ Offense
- ➢ Defense
- ➢ Special Teams
- ➢ Strength & Conditioning
- ➢ Sub-Varsity Programs
- ➢ Booster Club
- ➢ Player Development
- ➢ Practice
- ➢ Game Day
- ➢ Summer Schedule
- ➢ Injury Prevention/Management
- ➢ In-Season Weekend/Scouting
- ➢ Facilities & Equipment
- ➢ Technology use
- ➢ Community relations
- ➢ Relationships with other sports and programs in school
- ➢ Relationships with Administration

Then I would ask a few questions that did not fit this formula but still needed feedback:

➢ What are some things we need to buy this year?
➢ Who are some students in the building who are not playing but should?
➢ What are your strengths as a coach?
➢ What are your weaknesses as a coach?
➢ What are some things you personally want to work on in the coming year as a coach?
➢ Where do you see yourself in 5 years? 10 years?
➢ Any additional notes or comments

As an Athletic Director I made a survey and adapted it to all sports. This survey was sent to all coaches to complete at the end of the season. I believe in surveys. They give the person a chance to gather their thoughts and give honest feedback. Then I would follow these up with individual meetings to discuss results.

Do not be scared to modify a survey and send it to players, parents, or administrators. Sure, some of the feedback will be ridiculous or selfish but you can ignore that. I bet you will find that some of the feedback is positive and constructive. If you do not get your feelings hurt and stay focused on your vision, you may just become a better leader because of some of the comments!

Self-Evaluation: How do you do it?

- ✓ **Have a system to make notes** – you do not have to do it like I did, but have a system to take notes on what you can do better and then have a system to implement that plan.

- ✓ **Use surveys** – it is easier than it has ever been to create an online survey that can be completed and submitted. Take advantage of this valuable tool.

- ✓ **Follow up on surveys** – after the evaluation is complete, have an individual meeting with each coach and discuss their answers. It is not good enough to only gather the information. You must follow up on it.

Conclusion

Sid Maxwell taught me so many things about running the program and all aspects of coaching football. He had some great sayings. I stole many of them. Today, I imagine many of my players credit me for some sayings that I am sure were Coach Maxwell's first. One of my favorites was "we don't have any magic beans". We had to work. We had to get better all the time. You do not have time to sit around and wait for things to happen or act like you know it all and do not need to improve. Make a commitment to constant progress!

Now that you have learned the importance of building relationships, having a plan, communicating, being a good presenter, keeping your vision over your feelings, avoiding petty problems, focusing on what you have, and continued growth, you are finally ready for one of the hardest lessons of all: you will deal with things you never envisioned and you must step up….even when it's hard.

Lesson Nine:

Step up...even when it is hard

Honestly this may be the most difficult lesson to execute. It can start as simple as understanding when you become a leader, you will deal with things you NEVER imagined. When you put that leader title next to your name people will see you differently. The challenging part is that you do not always see yourself differently. They see you as the leader of the organization and when someone has a question or something happens, they all look to the leader to step up.

This can be as small as you will spend half of the day hearing about how "somebody" stole their helmet, "somebody" took their pads, "somebody" said we did not have practice tomorrow, etc. For the record...if anyone ever finds "somebody" please let me know. This guy has done a lot of damage!

I wish all the things you had to step up and deal with were that trivial. When I took over the team at Chapel Hill that had never had a winning season in school history and we won 9 games in my first year, I thought that was my biggest challenge as a head coach. I was sadly mistaken. Over the next several years I would deal with situations that I never dreamed would come about and for which there is no book or manual to help you.

Stepping up is hard. It is easier to avoid and deflect and it is difficult rise above. Stepping up is what true leaders do. There is a reason you only know some U.S. Presidents. Most of the ones you know from the past are due to them being in office when it was hard, and everyone looked to the leader to "step up." You must step up, even when it is hard to do! As a coach, you are leader of young men, other coaches, families, and even communities. You must step up when your people need you.

Here are the important factors:
- ✓ Step up in tough conversations
- ✓ Step up in tough decisions
- ✓ The most difficult situation

Step up in tough conversations

So often, leadership fails because of the ignoring of things that needed to be addressed. It is difficult to have tough conversations with people and always feels easier to avoid the issue entirely. While this may work in different aspects of your life, as a leader you must be the one to step up and have the hard conversations. Stepping up in tough conversations could involve the following:

➢ ***Disciplining a player*** – If you have a player that is not doing what they are supposed to do, you must have a conversation with them. This sounds simple but I have seen this not get addressed, especially if it is one of the better players. You must talk candidly to them and be clear with your disappointment and your expectations for the future. As challenging as it is, try to show empathy but do not let them "off the hook"

➢ ***Dealing with a parent that is upset*** – If you have an upset parent, it is best to confront the situation and not hide from it. Set up a time to talk to them. I always liked to set an appointment and not deal with it immediately after a practice or game. I would have an agenda and confront the issue.

➢ **Dealing with rumors or innuendo** – If I heard the principal, basketball coach, or band director was upset with me, I would call them. If I heard a teacher was upset about how we handled things, I would ask them about it. I dealt with rumor and innuendo head on. I did not get upset at them, I just confronted the issue and asked what we could do better or what suggestions they may have for improvement. It can always just be a misunderstanding. I found this method to be highly effective.

These conversations are when all the previous lessons merge to form a result. To make these tough conversations successful you must have:

1. A relationship with the person so you can talk to them candidly when they make selfish decisions and make them realize they can do better.
2. A plan in place so the expectations were clear.
3. Been a good communicator so they give you the benefit of the doubt.
4. A good presentation and deliver on your message in the tough conversation.
5. Kept the program's vision ahead of your feelings and not let your emotions take over
6. Avoided petty problems in the past so they know you mean business.
7. Focused on the positive over the course of your relationship.

8. Kept a positive outlook in your previous interactions.

If you have done all these things, these conversations have a much better chance to be successful. If you have not, they will be exponentially more difficult. Honestly, you can do all these things and still not have a successful conversation, but at least you did all you could.

Step up in tough decisions

Keep in mind when you accept a leadership title, it comes with some strings attached. You are going to have to make tough decisions. In a football game, I had to make the tough decisions like whether to go for it on 4th down or punt, go for one or two after a touchdown, decline or accept a penalty, etc. When you make those in-game decisions it is important to be decisive and confident. While these decisions can be tough, these were the "easier" of the hard decisions.

The toughest decisions are the ones that occur off the field or court. If you make some of these tougher decisions, make sure to include your supervisors. Do not let them be surprised to hear about these things from other people. The more support you get before everyone finds out, the better. Stepping up in tough decisions could involve the following:

➤ ***Dismissing a player from the team*** – For me, this was the most challenging of the tough conversations and decisions. I never wanted to give up on a kid. I tried hard to always give them a punishment that was tough but also gave them hope to be on the team. I knew dismissing anyone from the team was rarely the best thing for that individual. There are certain instances, however, where what is best for the team is just not the same as what is best for that individual. Occasionally, you must dismiss someone from the team to grow. Addition by subtraction. I would NEVER make these decisions in haste and I would never take them lightly. If I was divided, the tie should go to keeping the player on the team. Find a difficult punishment that allows them to stay in the program if possible, but if you can not grow as a team with this person on the team, you dismiss. Have a tough conversation with the athlete and let them know that you still care about them and will continue to wish them the best luck moving forward.

➤ ***Having to fire a coach*** – I was very fortunate that I worked with a lot of great coaches but there are situations where you would have to let a coach go. My two main gauges on coach retention was: Be loyal and show improvement. The main issue with coaches would be loyalty. If they are not loyal, it may create an unsolvable problem. If they are loyal and just not effective, give them another chance and keep working with them. Ultimately, the decision needs to be the same as with the player: Can the team move forward with this person? If the answer is no, you have to make a change. These are some of the worst conversations to have as it affects more than just the individual coach. If you must dismiss a coach, make sure that you have given ample time to improve and clear expectations. I hate seeing coaches get "surprised" with this information.

➤ **Leaving a job** – Coaches are notorious for asking for loyalty until it is their time to look elsewhere. There is nothing wrong with trying to advance your career, but there is a right way to leave a job. Be a leader, step up, and do it the right way if you need to leave. Talk to the players and be honest with them. Let them know that you loved working with them and this is a good move for you but you will miss them. Do not let them find out from their friend or on social media. If you are an assistant coach and you are leaving for another job, make sure the Head Coach knows. Do not let it be a shock to him if he gets a call from the new place. If you are a Head Coach, do the same for your Principal and Athletic Director. Do not let the principal be surprised by this news. You step up, walk in there, and tell them what is going on. This happens the wrong way far too often and relationships, memories, and legacies can be destroyed.

Tough Decisions/Conversations: How do you do it?

✓ **Recognize you are the leader** – it is hard to have to deal with tough situations, but since you assumed the leadership role you must do it.

✓ **Recognize the need for the conversation** – be aware and keep your eyes open to situations that need a tough conversation.

✓ **Ask yourself if you are doing this for vision or feelings** – these tough decisions should not be made lightly. They should align with your vision and plan and not be knee-jerk or emotional decisions.

✓ **Stay strong in your conviction** – It is easy to make excuses in your head for why certain behavior is acceptable and you avoid the tough conversation. This is easier in the short term but causes more damage to the program in the long term. Stay true to your conviction.

✓ **Get support from your supervisor** – keep your supervisors in the loop of the tough conversations and decisions. The less they are surprised with the better.

✓ **If possible, be empathetic as well** – empathy will go a long way in tough conversations. It is possible to be empathetic and stick to your guns.

The most difficult situation

There is no manual, book, or course that you take to prepare you for some of the most difficult situations that arise in coaching. None were more difficult for me than two events in 2017.

On March 11, 2017, I was in my basement working on spring football practice plans when my phone rang. It was our local law enforcement to let me know we had a player that had an accident. It did not look like he was going to survive the accident. As anyone who has been through this realizes, your heart sinks and you feel helpless. Jordan Simonds passed away in an automobile accident that day. Jordan was on the path to being a great player and was a leader on our team in his upcoming junior class.

I had never dealt with anything like this. As the leader of the program, our players and coaches looked to me to help grieve. I had no idea what to do. I wanted to be there for his family and our team but I had no idea how. We organized a community event the next evening and I spent all day at the field house. We saw our players and coaches as they dropped by through the day and we just grieved together. We saw Jordan's family and tried to be there for the them the best we could. I have never been more devastated for loss and prouder of our community at the same time. We came together and mourned Jordan.

Being the district Athletic Director as well as the Head Football Coach I was charged with organizing these events and speaking to the media. It was so difficult to speak about. Jordan was a team leader and our players were devastated. As a group, all of us wanted to find as many ways as possible to honor Jordan's memory. We had a flag made to run out of the banner with at games, we retired his number 39, and took the jersey with us on the road. We left his locker the same and put plexiglass on it. These were all things the players wanted to do, and I was so proud of them. I try to stay in touch with Jordan's family. I know the pain never goes away and there is not a week that goes by that I do not think about the loss of Jordan. I knew it was the hardest thing I had gone through in my life at the time and could not imagine what it was like for his family. I hope we did all we could to honor him.

On October 6, 2017, almost seven months later, we traveled to Southeast Whitfield High School in Dalton, Georgia for a region game. We had the better team and were winning at halftime, but I was in a bad mood because we had not ended the half like I wanted. I was on my way to talk to the team when our principal, Chris Wallace, stopped me and said he needed to talk to me. As I mentioned earlier, Chris and I are friends and he had never interrupted me in a game so I knew it must be important, but I am sure the look on my face was not a pleasant one. He proceeded to tell me that one of our younger players not on the trip, Shawn Mask, had passed away in an accident. I have never felt so small. I had let the pettiness of winning get me in a bad mood and now all the emotions of losing another young man came back. We lost another young man who has a family and friends. All I could think about was how hard this would be on our players. We decided we would tell them after the game. I do not remember one thing from that 2nd half other than we won the game. The other coaches did not know but I am sure they thought something was wrong with me as I was not acting like myself.

After every game I coached in, we would shake hands with the other team and gather on our side of the field where I would address the team. Some coaches like to do it in the locker room, but I always liked to do it there and then we turned them loose to do their post-game responsibilities and see family and friends. I have many times had to really think hard about what to say after a tough loss, as these times can be critical to program development, but I had NEVER been prepared for the message I was about to deliver. I did the best I could to tell them their friend was no longer with us and we would need to come together again, as a team, to honor Shawn and his memory. Delivering this message to the team was devastating for me, but as the leader, I had to do it. Immediately, everyone was crushed. Shawn had great potential. Since then, we have tried to honor him in the same ways and be there for his family.

Dealing with two teenage deaths in seven months on your team will change anyone's perspective. As the leader, I had to step up and help with these issues even when they were exceptionally difficult for me as a person. These are times that you will never be prepared.

Those two deaths really took a toll on our 2017 team. We were already playing a lot of young players but we did start the year 4-2. After Shawn's death, we struggled and ended up finishing fourth in our region and losing in the first round of the state playoffs. The region champ, Ridgeland, beat us late in the season. The next week we were preparing for our senior night against Lafayette. Ridgeland had pushed our young team around and they were discouraged. I told them to remember this moment. We were going to spend all week honoring our seniors and getting them a win on Friday night against Lafayette. Their senior year had been dominated by losing two teammates. I told the team that one year from that week, in 2018, we were going to have senior night against Ridgeland at our stadium and it was going to be for the region championship

10 Lessons in Coaching

and we were going to win it. We were going to win it for those 2017 seniors, the 2018 team, and for Jordan and Shawn.

I am sure our players gave no real thought to that speech until I brought it up when we were playing Ridgeland for the region championship on senior night in 2018. I asked them if they remembered my prediction the year before. Most of them did. They had worked so hard that year to honor themselves, their community, and their fallen teammates. We now ran out of the banner with flags for Jordan and Shawn. We talked about them often. We won that game against Ridgeland and claimed the region championship and an undefeated regular season. It was so much fun! It felt like Jordan and Shawn were with us all the way!

Conclusion

Leading our program through the deaths of two of our players and finding a way to navigate a 10-0 season with the classmates of these two young men is my proudest accomplishment. The toughness and love that our team had for each other after these experiences is not something I am sure I will ever find again. I am grateful to have been a part of it.

Leadership can be tough. A lot of people think football coaches just get Gatorade dumped on them and yell and scream a lot. This is not what it is all about. You must navigate some

140

of the most difficult situations. Situations that can come out of nowhere that you did not create and that will totally change the course of your program and career. It is all part of life as a leader. You do not control these things popping up, but you do control how you navigate them.

Now we can move on to the final lesson. Once you realize there are going to be VERY tough situations that you have to handle, many of which you did not create, you need to understand to have fun. Regardless of all the chaos, there should still be a place for fun!

Lesson Ten:

Have fun and make it fun

I hope the first nine chapters helped you realize how difficult it can be to put pieces together to make the leadership puzzle. It can be such a challenging job, but it is worth it! You must find ways to have fun and make it fun! This is the advice I would give my younger self more than any other and that is why I chose to make it the final lesson. Even with all the ups and downs it is truly an honor to be the leader of a program. It is also your job to make it fun.

Any of our former players can finish this sentence: "We want you to have fun and all, but it's only fun

_____". They would all say, "when you win!"   I said that so many times. The truth is that is not a great statement. I often made it only fun when we won. That was a huge mistake. It should always be fun. It is a blessing to be able to be a part of a team. I think my heart was in the right place. I usually followed that statement up with some talk about that is why we must execute better or something that will help us win and have some more fun. There was nothing wrong with telling the players we needed better execution, I just am not sure I should have correlated that to fun.

Dr. Flatt, my brother Michael, and I do a podcast: Parker Resources Podcast. We started it to stay involved and it has taken off. We have interviewed tons of great coaches. Most of them vastly more successful than we were. The common theme is that winning is not what made them feel better. It was the relationships they built over time. All of them say that after you win a first championship, you almost get a feeling of "this is it?" Then you feel like you have to win a championship again and again and again or it is a failure. This does not mean we do not want to win. Winning is great and it can lead to so many other positive things in your program. You just have to have fun and make it a fun experience first. Do not make winning first; create a fun atmosphere.

Making it fun can have a positive impact on so many things. Making the program so fun players go home talking about how much fun they have. This is an enormously powerful tool. If you want to make your program great, you need to get ahead of as many problems as possible. Players going home and talking about having fun on your team is a great place to start!

Here are the important factors:
- ✓ Make your group special
- ✓ Be enthusiastic
- ✓ Run with the organic themes
- ✓ Family atmosphere (for real!)

Make your group special

Whatever you are doing, make it special! If you are the Freshman coach, be the best freshman coach around and make those freshmen feel like they are special. This is a trait I saw in many good coaches. Offensive Line coaches seem to be the best at this, but all groups on the team should work to make their group special. Give out some small awards daily, have group dinners, and any other team-building thing you can think of to make your group special. We took this mantra for the entire team as well.

<u>Here are some ways we tried to make it special</u>
- ✓ **Summer party** – we had big party for players at the end of each summer. We would get some inflatables and other toys and let them have fun. We would eat and give out summer awards. Then we would have a drawing for prizes. We would give out raffle tickets based on how

many summer workouts you made and if you made your strength and speed goals for the year. Obviously, the more tickets, the more chance to win. We gave away some big gift cards and always had a few big prizes with a lot of little ones.

✓ **Parent Meetings** – we would have Freshman and Senior parent meetings. Especially at the freshman meetings we would have a drawing for door prizes, feed them, and make it a fun atmosphere.

✓ **Theme Days** – when possible, we tried to have a theme for the day. It could be something pertaining to the team like Tough Monday or it could be something fun. Our summer Tuesdays were "Tank Top Tuesday" and even the coaches were encouraged to wear a Tank Top. The players loved this!

✓ **Mother's Day** – Mother's Day weekend usually fell during our spring practice. We would invite the moms to the end of practice. We would have food for them and give them a rose. We would make a short video of the players saying how much they loved their moms and show it to them.

✓ **Guest speakers** – we would always bring back old players to talk to the team. Sometimes it was someone who played forty years earlier. We loved having guest speakers talk to our team about what playing for our program meant to them. We would also invite the administration and coaches of other sports to address the team at some point in the year.

✓ **Teacher captains** – At home games, we would let seniors pick a favorite teacher and give that teacher an away game jersey with the players number to wear to school on Friday. This was a way they could show their support. Those would be our honorary "teacher captains" for the game. This was a fun opporutnity to get support in the building and make it feel special.

✓ **Banquet Scholarships** – I did not believe in doing a lot of awards at the banquet. Football is a sport that lends to teamwork. For me, it was hard to pick "Receiver of the Year" and stuff like that. We had a few key awards that were won through merit (GPA, strength training) and then we honored our seniors. Sheryl Messner, our booster club Treasurer the entire time I was at Pickens and an amazing person, came up with the idea for Touchdown Club Scholarships. We would award scholarships sent to their school for all seniors who played all four years, had no major discipline issues, and wrote an essay stating what playing football meant to them. This was a huge success. We used the money people typically spend on awards plus a little more we would solicit and divided it among the seniors that qualified. All our players that qualified at Pickens got at least $500 toward their first year of college!

Be enthusiastic

Enthusiasm breeds enthusiasm. I have heard that said many times, but I witnessed it occur over the years at practice. We needed our coaches to make a personal choice to bring some enthusiasm to whatever we were doing. When the coaches brought enthusiasm, the players did too. When the coaches were dragging, the players did too. It can not be fake enthusiasm. You must be genuine and show your love for the game.

Here are some ways we worked to be enthusiastic

- ✓ **Personal choice** – each coach must make a personal choice to have fun and be enthusiastic at practice. This must happen before anything else. Everything can be fun if you have the right attitude.

- ✓ **Ending practice with fun** – we would occasionally let a lineman catch a punt and if he caught it there would be no conditioning. You have never seen so many people cheering on their teammate!

- ✓ **Reverse practice** – every now and then (not often) we would start practice with a reverse practice and let the lineman do the backs/receivers drills like Pat & Go and let the backs/receivers do the lineman drills. It was not fundamentally helpful, but the players loved it!

- ✓ **Practice Shaking hands** – enthusiasm can work both ways: if practice is dragging and getting excited does not help, you may have to get mad. I would occasionally stop practice if it were dragging and make everyone shake hands like it was the end of the game. I would tell them we were probably going to get beat if we did not bring more energy, so we just needed to practice shaking hands and saying "good game". While tremendously sarcastic, it did seem to work. After we practiced shaking hands, we usually came back with some energy and excitement.

Run with the organic themes

The best teams I have been on have had common themes that carried them throughout the season. Some of these were articulate and passionate, and some were just silly. The best coaches find a way to use anything they can to have a common theme for the season. The best themes are the organic themes.

In 2011 our team carried a stuffed Giraffe to every game. I can not even remember how this started. I think one of our team leaders brought it to practice as a joke and we had a good practice, so we told him to bring it back. We took it to the game, and we won. We told him to bring it next week. Before you know it, the Giraffe is a key member of the sideline. He had his own spot to sit and watch and after we made big plays, players would come to the sideline and hold up the giraffe. It was crazy and wonderful at the same time. As a coach, it was my job to recognize that organic fun theme and support it. I started talking about the Giraffe too. We won our sub-region championship.

We knew before the season our 2018 Pickens team had a chance to be good. We played a lot of young guys the year before. For whatever reason, we had started the previous couple years 1-1 after 2 games. Going into that year, no player had even started the year 2-0 in varsity football. Leading up to the 2nd game of the season, I asked the team everyday to "raise your hand if you have ever been 2-0 in varsity football" and only coaches would raise their hand. They got so tired of me doing it that week that after we won the game to go to 2-0, they all started yelling at me about raising their hand. They were so excited. So, when we settled down, I told them to "raise your hand if you have ever been 3-0". It caught on. My standard first line when addressing the team after a win that year was to raise my hand and ask the question for that week and we would all celebrate by raising our hands. Then we would talk about doing it the next week. I did not intend for that to be a season-long theme, but it became a great one.

Look for the opportunities to have your giraffe and fun saying this coming season. If you pay attention, some organic themes are out there!

Family atmosphere (for real!)

I think a lot of people want a family atmosphere but to really have fun and make it fun you must create a real family atmosphere on your team. I felt like the best way to do that was to have it with the coaches. If we all got along great and had a great time out there it would permeate into the players. We always had good fellowship in the coaches' office. This is important to having fun. Coaches need to work hard and feel like they are making meaningful contributions to the team.

At Chapel Hill, we did not have a large booster club. If we won, we would pool some money together ourselves and get some "victory pizza" for the coaches. It turned into a fun tradition! Take any chance you can to make your own "family" traditions and grow the program!

We created a family atmosphere at Pickens by including everyone. My friend, Kyle Rasco served many roles in our program. He was the Athletic Trainer but also served as the leader of the managers. We usually had around 20 managers that were a big part of the team culture. Kyle also served as the resident comedian in the field house!

If you do not think your program matters to the players, you are wrong! Regardless of your success level, your program matters to the young people that make up the roster. This became evident to me through our scholarship program. Players had to write a paper about what football meant to them to get the scholarship. I was always blown away by what the seniors would write in these papers. I saved all of them and still have them today.

Your program already matters…make it a family atmosphere and make it special!

Conclusion

Coaching and playing is too much work to not be fun. Take some time to think about ways to enjoy the journey.

My last bit of advice is this…..do not just make it fun for everyone else – have some fun yourself! I wish I would have had more fun with some of our earlier teams. It is alright to have a little fun and enjoy yourself!

Epilogue

I hope it did not come across like I have all the answers as a coach. All these lessons were learned the hard way. It is also important to note that these will not be the last lessons I will learn. I know there are many more lessons that I will need to learn in the future.

All of this is my opinion. It is an educated opinion, but I feel a need to state that there a plenty of ways to be successful. If someone disagrees with my method of doing anything in this book, that is fine. Do not read any of this as me saying it is absolute and there are no exceptions.

Everything in this book is hard to do. If you think any of this is easy, you are going to be mistaken. If you think any of this is "too" hard, you are in the wrong profession. You can do it! No one said it would be easy to be successful. Success takes doing things that others will not do.

Take these lessons and apply them to your career. They may be helpful to any coach of any sports, athletic directors, or leaders of any kind. Take control of your situation and use these ten lessons I learned over the years to help you succeed!

Acknowledgments

I would like to thank a lot of people for helping me with this project. My family has been so instrumental in my career. I am writing this in part for my daughters to have a frame of reference for what their father did for a large portion of his life. My wife Kimberly has been helpful in writing this book as she has served as an editor and a friend to help me put my thoughts down on paper.

The families of Jordan Simonds and Shawn Mask were gracious enough to grant me permission to talk about their sons in this book. As you can imagine that was the hardest part to write. The profound impact those two young men and their families have had on me is enormous.

Coaching is such as special profession in part due to the relationships you build with your colleagues. I would like to thank the guys that worked in the field house with me over the years. Many of them were gracious enough to help me with this project. Michael Parker, Chad Flatt, Sam Wigington, Ty Maxwell, Bo Page, Ben Ford, Matt Ely, Brad Carroll, Adam Wharton, Louis Daniel, Stephen Hunter, Jeff Nelson, Kyle Rasco, Grant Myers, and many more helped me along the way with this process and have been great friends to me over the years.

I would like to thank all the administrators and direct supervisors I have had over the years. I consider myself extremely fortunate to have been around many good leaders and this has allowed me to become a better leader. Doe Kirkland, Sid Maxwell, Jason Branch, Sean Kelly, Eddie McDonald, Chris LeMieux, Shane Purdy, Chris Wallace, Lula Mae Perry, Carlton Wilson and Charles Webb all helped mold me into a better worker and teammate and I am sincerely thankful.

Finally, I would like to thank all the players over the years that referred to me as "Coach". While I was not always the easiest guy in the world to deal with, I assure you I always wanted what was best for you and my intentions were to make you as good as you could be. I have been privileged to coach thousands of young men. I did not take that responsibility lightly. I enjoyed being your coach and I hope I was able to help you in some capacity and will be there for you in the future if you need me.

About the Author

Chris Parker served as a Head Football Coach, Athletic Director, and school District Athletic Director for many years. He was the Head Football Coach at Chapel Hill High School in Douglasville, GA from 2008-11 and Pickens High School in Jasper, GA from 2012-18. He took over both schools when they were struggling and turned them into winning programs. Teams at both schools set school records for wins, playoff appearances, and playoff production. He led the best seasons in school history at both schools and helped them both win their first state playoff game in school history.

As Athletic Director of Pickens County Schools, Coach Parker presided over all sports programs in the district. During his time as District AD, the district pursued many capital improvements to the athletic facilities, set new highs for money raised, championships, and scholarship athletes.

Coach Parker has been a speaker at clinics nationally and has been a writer for USA Football and X&O Labs. He has been active in the Georgia Elite Classic All-Star Game, the Georgia Athletic Coaches Association, the Georgia Athletic Directors Association, and the American Football Coaches Association. He has been awarded many Coach of the Year awards and was named the Marine Corps' 2017 Semper Fi

Award winner for the Southeast United States for work on and off the field.

He is currently the Director of Human Resources for the Pickens County School District. He lives in Talking Rock, GA with his wife Kimberly and daughters, Ellie & Kate. Coach Parker also acts as a consultant for coaches and Athletic Directors through Parker & Co Resources, LLC. You can follow Coach Parker on social media and at http://www.parkerresources.org.